Convincing a Puzzled World
that God Sent His Son

"THAT THEY MAY BE ONE"

JESUS

by
Thomas Donn Twitchell

Logos International
Plainfield, New Jersey

All Scripture references, unless otherwise noted, are taken from the Revised Standard Version of the Bible.

Dedicated to
Jesus in all the
family of our Father

Pam, Binky & James

Do a family we love and appreciate so dearly and to whom we feel so close and loving a bond; to the continual inspiration you are in your awe, sensitivity and deep love for life and your courage and determination against death; to your love for us that is so pure and space filled whether we are up or sinking down; we give this part of our lives with all our love & thanksgiving. Truth & duty

Contents

Part I: My Spiritual Journey—An Expression of
Growing Unity

Part II: Unity Within the Body of Christ

Part III: Unity of the Body of Christ in the World

Appendix: The First New England Regional
         Conference of Catholic Charismatics

Foreword

Maybe I'm prejudiced, but I think this is a rather important book. As I read it, I realized anew that Tom Twitchell and I are very close brothers with similar histories: involvement in social action in the inner city and active participation in the renewal. As I read of his journey, I relived and reflected afresh on my own, and received new insights, new depths. I became excited and angry; I wept and said, "Right on." I simply couldn't put the book down. I ended up feeling convinced that the Spirit is speaking here a powerful message.

Tom Twitchell is a beautiful man who exudes the love of Jesus. This definitely is his dominant characteristic. As a result he can say some very hard things, some very indicting things, and he does, but you are aware that they come right from the heart of Jesus. For example, "The truth of pentecostals will be squandered unless the means [of getting it across] are the same as the end—the love of Jesus, firm to be sure but always humble. . . . I'm beginning to see that while this movement is here to stay it is meant to lead us elsewhere and the basic criticism of the [charismatic] movement is that it too easily falls into the trap of attempting to renew every tradition in its path, soon succumbs to its own law, and thereby loses the cutting edge of the Spirit. . . ."

There lies deep in Tom's loving personality the passion of the prophet with a vision. He does not divert from it for an instant. This has caused deep pain and disappointment as he has seen the vision watered down, forgotten, rejected. I can remember when Tom was a little behind if not against the charismatic renewal; now I wonder if his pain doesn't come mainly from being ahead of most of it. When he heard the Lord at Atlantic City in 1976, and in Kansas City in 1977, he literally sold all he had to buy the vision. Now he stands rather lonely but undaunted, a shining witness that God did indeed speak an important word, a word still largely unheard.

The sections of the book that deal with personal purification are exquisite. Rarely have I seen a desert experience or a "night of the soul" so beautifully described. Many write of the glories of the renewal. Few have written of the even more powerful experiences of the charismatic cross. I am left with the very definite impression that this "seed fallen into the ground and dying is going to bear very much fruit."

The book is full of precious insights. Let me share a few. "The word used to be: 'Hang in there, endure, grow in patience and understanding!' Now I believe the word is a different one: 'Now churches, rise up; accept your resurrection; live in radical faith; band together in truth, wisdom and discernment. You have all the gifts you need. Be courageous and follow the Spirit. Let no tradition or enemy, visible or invisible, stop you. You are being prepared for battle. Strip down. Exercise the authority I have given you. . . . Be willing to go where you have not gone before. Be willing to go beyond your experience. Others were called before you. Many have not listened. The time is short but it is not too late. . . .' "

And here's another: "Renewal, baptism in the Holy Spirit, a deepening love and devotion for Jesus . . . ultimately will not, as we are so often criticized for, cause us to withdraw from the world and its concerns. The difference is a joyful, enduring Christian reaching out to the man in the gutter, who will not withdraw when the going gets rough, as opposed to the tired, unrefreshed

Christian who in time will falter under the burden of another man in the gutter."

Still another is where Tom eloquently talks of the tensions between authority, submission, the building of the body, on the one hand—all of which are very valid concerns—and on the other hand the universal commission of Jesus to evangelize the world along with the universal call to ministry. Both have to happen. As a true Presbyterian, the author rightly feels that the second is often given short shrift. He writes: "In many places it became so entrenched to go home and die in the church body we were part of that we did just that—we died. The Lord's Spirit moved on and we were still dying."

There are some powerful indictments from this loving yet bold prophet on society, churches, social activists, charismatic renewal, the council of churches. However, these criticisms are never merely negative, but always constructive and redeeming. Tom Twitchell is a man of unity from the top of his head to the tip of his toes. It comes across. His life is on the line to prove it and the record speaks for itself.

There are a couple of points on which Tom and I disagree. One is his feeling that there is no longer any time to build Catholic bridges, Presbyterian bridges, Lutheran bridges, etc., but that we must all cross whatever bridges there are. I think Tom is a bit impatient here. I feel we must do both. I particularly disagree and see as unfortunate the witness of the Catholic priest who went ahead of his bishop in concelebrating an ecumenical Eucharist. I can only see that as hurting the cause. We must be in a hurry, yes, but always under obedience.

The other difference I feel is this. God does give a double portion of His Spirit to ecumenical activities today. I have witnessed this with Tom. However, I feel that we need to have a greater respect for the gifts of the Spirit. For example, God will heal at an ecumenical service, yes. But He will heal even more powerfully when we observe carefully where the gifts of healing are and go there. There is power in doing things ecumenically. There is even more power in recognizing God's gifts and rallying around them. Now when the two of these truths are put together, watch out!

"THAT THEY MAY BE ONE"

In conclusion, I want to affirm that Tom Twitchell is a prophet ahead of his time. Yes, but there is a lady right with him all the way, a lady who has often led him—his wife, Judy. They are a beautiful team who in their relationship already bespeak the unity these pages foretell.

John Randall

Acknowledgments

Above all, I would like to express my thanks to the Lord. I continually return thanks to Him for my mom and dad and brother and his family who have given me an abundance and constancy of love. I thank Him for my wife, Judy, and her tender, understanding and sacrificial love and for our children who have always patiently and trustingly loved me—especially during the formation and writing of this book.

Judy and I are one and we continue to grow together in the love He has for us. Her editing and suggestions throughout this book have been God's precious gifts.

I thank Him for Judy's mom and dad who loved me and took me as their son from the very beginning.

I also express my gratitude to Him for Valerie Carleton who graciously sat with our children in the very first days of writing and for Judy's sister and her husband and family, the Obadals, who made their home available to us while the major portion of the book was being written. I thank the Lord for Tom Carleton who painstakingly typed the manuscript and for Cathy White who gave special encouragement along the way. I thank Him for Logos, His precious servant in spreading the Word. And finally, I offer my

"THAT THEY MAY BE ONE"

thanks to Him for all the people on each page of the book, especially for all the times they shared their love not only with me but also with the world He so deeply and completely loves.

Introduction

"The Lord is doing a new thing!" How frequently we have heard this message from so many voices. How deeply and adventurously it has stretched our imaginations. What is the Lord doing? How is He doing it? What is our part?

He has given us some answers. The Lord, changeless for all time, is moving in perfect timing to fulfill promises He has made to His people. Together, we have received a new vision of history and of an approaching new era—of the Spirit being poured out on all flesh, of a new evangelism as the body of Christ comes together to praise, of a yet unattained, exciting unity, of a revival that will sweep the world, of the restoration of Israel and "cities on the hill" all over the world, of the holistic unity of ourselves with God, of unity within ourselves and with others in every endeavor from prayer to family life, from work to fellowship, from singing to suffering, of so many other wonderful blessings.

The Lord takes His perfect time, yet works so fast, to prepare us to receive even the smallest part of His vision. This book deals with His preparation and life in me and how it led to our present vision and hope that simply believes and confesses that we stand on the threshold of an adventure in the Christian world—the Father's answer to Jesus' prayer in John 17. It shares the pain we have experienced in preparation to be the sons and daughters of one Father within one family, possessing this hope. We await His glory with new hearts and eyes.

My spirit is one with this call to unity and I would like to share with you now, from the beginning, the way the Lord chose to work toward this end in my life. It is the deep within Him calling to that which is deep within all of us who are moved by Jesus' prayer for unity.

> *Why are you cast down, O my soul,*
> *and why are you disquieted within me?*
> *Hope in God; for I shall again praise him,*
> *my help and my God.*

> *My soul is cast down within me,*
> *therefore I remember thee*
> *from the land of Jordan and of Hermon,*
> *from Mount Mizar.*
> *Deep calls to deep*
> *at the thunder of thy cataracts;*
> *all thy waves and thy billows*
> *have gone over me. (Ps. 42:5-7)*

PART I:

My Spiritual Journey—
An Expression of Growing
Unity

1

Raised Up in Love—
God, the Creator

Follow the pattern of the sound words which you have heard
from me, in the faith and love which are in Christ Jesus; guard
the truth that has been entrusted to you by the Holy Spirit who
dwells within us. (2 Tim. 1:13-14)

It was a beautiful June evening. The birds sang hushed melodies
in the warmth of the setting sun. The air was clear and a gentle
breeze swept around us as we prepared to go to church. This night
was to be more memorable than my school graduations, award
banquets, military balls, and drum corps field contests. The Rev.
Dr. Stanley Gutelius who had baptized my mother fifty-three years
before and joined her in marriage to my father nineteen years later
was to give me my charge and to pray the ordination prayer. Rev.
Clinton Kenney, a dear friend from my early days of church camp
conferences, was to preach the sermon. Seminary graduation had
just been a month before and my first job as assistant pastor awaited
me the next week at the First Presbyterian Church of Hagerstown,
Maryland. This was the night of my ordination into the Christian
ministry, an occasion I had been preparing for all my life. It would
take place in the church, amidst the congregation I had known
since I was four years old.

As we left the beautiful old home and grounds of my boyhood
and drove down the familiar streets, memories swept across my
mind along with a sense of awesomeness about this night when
many of my seminary classmates were also being ordained in home

churches to be sent to the farthest corners of the world. I was proud of them. I was proud of my mom and dad and I was proud of Judy, my wife. I was proud of myself. School had not been easy for me but in the contest with the ivy halls I had won, fair and square. I now had two degrees in hand and after this night, a commission, for which the degrees were necessary. And I had sufficiently proved in the trials of ordination two weeks previously that I would be enough of a credit to my church and her Lord, Jesus Christ, that this night, ruling and teaching elders would lay on hands and charge me with fidelity to the faith, a true and pure witness to Jesus Christ, His love and His church.

As Dr. Gutelius spoke, I imagined him taking my mother when she was a baby from my grandmother's arms and baptizing her as was his charge and holding her close to himself just as Jesus would have done and claiming her, her children and her children's children for the kingdom of God and His Christ. He was a kind and grace-filled gentleman with a twinkle in his eye, a ready smile, and always an eloquent word to give. In his gentleness and age, he was an awesome and powerful figure, yet really very humble and down to earth. I was glad he had been a part of my mother's and grandparents' lives, and that he was the man who had joined my parents in marriage. On this evening he could share three generations of joy. When he married my parents, he had brought together two people who would deeply love their children. Out of their love for each other, they provided, with devoted hearts, the very best home they could for their two sons. We were a fairly traditional family. Mom and dad believed in fidelity to each other and were always true to one another. They believed in planning for their children so my brother Warren was born three and one-half years after their marriage day and I came along five and one-half years after Warren. Dad believed he was the breadwinner and worked hard throughout his career to provide a comfortable home for his family, a good education for his sons, a secure life for all of us. Mom was always home—a very present, active, loving participant in all the days of our growing up. They poured so much of their lives for Warren and me that sometimes they had little time for each other, but we were the jewels in their crown of life

4

and they were always willing to sacrifice for our well-being.

We did everything together as a family. We were taught family life was a golden dream, always worth pursuing. We were taught to be proud of our parents and to have high standards for ourselves. Mom and dad were always proud of our accomplishments and disappointed at our failures. They made sure we were included in most of what they did around home and, though we knew less about dad's work, we were indeed proud that he was our dad. He's a gentle man ready to give and help wherever he can and we learned that gentleness and caring were good things. We knew and enjoyed most of our parents' friends and were often included in grown-up discussions.

Each week we saw all of our grandparents and most of our aunts, uncles and cousins who would gather at the old homestead. They would literally come just for the fun of it. And for many years, mom, dad, Warren and I would go to the movies on Friday nights, and come home to have ice cream sundaes or root beer floats at the kitchen table. If the night was pleasant, we would go out on the swing in our large back yard where we would talk on into the deep of the night. I remember the plans we used to make on the old double swing.

We were sure that after college, which had been planned for both Warren and me, Warren would come home, build a house next door, find a wife and settle down. I would come home, reconstruct the old barn that was on our second acre, find a wife and settle down too. (Concerning our going to college, dad had told Warren and me about a warm summer day following his high school graduation from a one-room schoolhouse in 1926. On this day my grandfather put him in the car and they drove thirty miles to the Rochester Institute of Technology. Grandpa told him, "I've enrolled you here for your first year of college. After your year here you may go to any college you wish and I will pay your way. There's only one stipulation—you must do the same for your children." Dad never knew he was going to college until this day but he promised his father he would reciprocate. He went on to the University of Pennsylvania, then to Syracuse University, becoming one of five graduates from the School of Architecture in

1931. When he got his first job, he began saving money for his yet unborn sons' educations. He continued to do so throughout his career.) Though Warren did indeed bring his wife home and move another old home next door and live there for a number of years, I never reconstructed the barn, for my young bride and I were destined to travel a different road.

With this love as my foundation, I grew in my sensitivity toward God who had given me every good thing in life. I grew in my thankfulness for all the love I knew from my parents, my brother, my grandparents, aunts and uncles. I grew in thankfulness for all my good friends and the many opportunities that lay at my feet. It was in this sense of thanksgiving that I began to open to the call of God, feeling rather determined at the age of eight or nine that I wanted to repay Him for all He had done for me.

Now my mind reflected on Rev. Harold W. Estes who had been my pastor for the last fifteen years. He and his wife, Polly, had been our good friends for many years while he pastored the church I grew up in. Our family again was very active in the church's life and it was my second home. "I wish I had a nickel," as the old saying goes, for every time I entered the parsonage next door to the church and was greeted as one of the family. In that home I would often find friends from school and for many months we would hold weekly band practice there for the little band we knew would outshine Glen Miller's but, in the end, we never actually performed for an audience. As early thoughts of ministry entered my mind, I would speak them to Harold. He would listen and be encouraging but he never tried to push me. He knew it was very early for any real decision but he left me with one very memorable thought in those early years and he would always express it to me by saying there is no more satisfying or wonderful work than the ministry. It is the highest calling and profession of God—greater than being a king or president. Later, of course, he would counsel me more deeply as the decision became actual. For now, however, it would remain a dream, the only one I really ever had for my life's work.

And now Clint Kenney was preaching. I remembered a

particularly solemn and quiet moment from our past which he and I shared with scores of others. My memory recalled a totally dark night at summer camp and it was beginning to chill. Inside the lodge, we watched silently as more and more people lighted candles from the persons next to them. Young faces began to brighten and smiles of love and friendship emerged. It was our last night together, having discovered each other all through the previous week, reaching our hearts and hands into one another's growing lives. All of us at camp had enjoyed every moment of our shared time. The fears of making new friends and running new risks had subsided in the first few hours after arriving at camp and we soon became fast friends. Now we were sad it was all about to end. The next morning would find us all wending our way back home having to adjust again to another world that would only be able to reflect upon these days and nights of magic in our lives. I had been to camp before and would go again but this last night of church camp in the Bristol Hills, adjacent to Canandaigua Lake in upstate New York, would be unlike any other I would know. Like many of our vespers around lighted fires outside, it was charged with an expectant faith, a sense of eternal things, an awe of God. Tonight, inside, we would also share the Lord's table with each other and Him. The white, painted wooden tables we had eaten on all week were now placed in the form of a cross that traversed the entire length and breadth of the huge rustic lodge. The center of the cross-shaped table was covered with pine bows along its full length and width that we had all collected in the afternoon. From this cross, together we received the Lord's Supper and were now lighting small candles from the center of our human circle outward. We sang, "This little light of mine; I'm going to let it shine. . . ." Then the officiating minister sensitively prayed, "Lord, please touch these young people with your call. Some you are calling to service in your church as ministers. Lord, please give them, especially now, the touch of your hand and warmth of your love as you lead them into full-time service for you." A prayer similar to this was probably given each year I attended our presbytery camp of the Genesee Valley but this year it stood out because I knew God was calling me. Though this was only one step in a developing call of God upon my life, it was one He allowed me to specifically recognize.

It was very good to have Clint preach the sermon at my ordination. After I met him at camp he too became a friend of the family and we were to see one another often. He, other ministers, all my teachers and many wonderful friends were to provide a childhood full of shining white knights. I grew up among the salt of the earth and was continually surrounded with love and affirmation. The church of the forties and fifties was quiet, unshaken, unchallenged; it was inspirational, studious, peaceful, asleep. She sent fewer sons into the ranks of ministry than she had before or after, but we were to become tested sons for service in a church which now battles on every front, a church which now finds the very breath of Christ in invisible places, a church whose foundations have been rocked to the very touchstone, a church which will yet dramatically change in the years ahead for those who have the eyes to see and ears to hear.

My childhood, though filled with unusual love, lots of laughter and fun, a lot of normal things and activities that attend growing up, was also very serious and shrouded in a radical sense of integrity both of which I see now to be gifts of preparation for these times when our Lord Jesus turns a serious countenance toward us and issues an unmistakable command for integrity, integration, unity, holism with ourselves, with our Creator God, with our loved ones close to us, with the body which is His throughout the world. Integrity defies that this must come at any cost, any compromise for it must come integrally. The only integrator is Jesus Christ who by the power of His Holy Spirit must act with integrity alone. He will yet find a people who will simply love Him and each other.

The service of ordination was over. We went home with our family and friends to fellowship together in rooms I would not often see again but which had silently watched as a boy grew up under the loving watchful care of his God and who had now made Him one with Him by His love.

Dear Father, I could never thank you enough for all the beautiful ways in which you have loved me. You placed me in a home where you knew I would learn the faithful, gentle, provisional love of a father; the wise, nurturing, patient, forgiving love of a mother; the strong, ever-ready, self-sacrificing love of a brother. You allowed me to know well all my grandparents, aunts, uncles and cousins. You gave me many supportive friends and acquaintances at all times and in every place. You know the thanksgiving I hold deep in my heart. Forgive me, Father, where I have failed the love of those you set before me to raise me up. And, Father, I pray through Jesus for all families, that they may increasingly know the wonders of your love for them and become increasingly set free to love each other through your love. Amen.

2

My Friend John—
Jesus, My Savior

Jesus said to him, "Have you believed because you have seen me? Blessed are those who have not seen and yet believe." (John 20:29)

Jesus said to him, "If it is my will that he remain until I come, what is that to you?" (John 21:22)

It was Thanksgiving time, 1964. In a cathartic way, I was looking forward to reliving the first anniversary of President Kennedy's assassination. The year before, while I was in seminary in Richmond, Virginia, as the news of his assassination began to have its full impact, I was virtually immobilized in tears for days. I hadn't realized how much hope and love I had placed in John Kennedy for a good future until he was gone. I wept as though I had lost my own brother. I was resentful and confused about the South I was in at that time where people could hold office parties the day of his assassination and school children in Richmond could clap with glee when they heard the news of his death. He had given me a hope beyond the hypocrisy of the late fifties and early sixties that had victimized so many of us who grew up in those days after World War II. Our hearts were one with social justice and we were on fire to rid the world of any injustice. Rightly or wrongly, we had placed great hope in the Kennedy administration being able to bring about deeply sought-after rights of oppressed peoples and for us it was Camelot. I suppose that was all a part of the catharsis I expected in November of 1964 but it was to come in an entirely different way.

I had a very close friend while I was growing up, who had also planned to become a minister. We separated in our college years and, while I pursued my originally intended course of preparation for the ministry, he changed his direction and decided to become an engineer. By 1964, he was married, as was I, and had begun work on his first job. News came a week prior to Thanksgiving that he had been killed in a freak automobile accident in Ohio. We decided to go immediately, as I felt I could be of some help to the family and couldn't conceive of myself not being there. We drove all night and arrived the next morning at the hospital where they had taken him. His wife was being hospitalized for minor injuries so we met with her and his family who had also just arrived. I had embarked on a spiritual journey that was to change my life and become the foundation of my current understanding of Jesus' love.

My friend had always loved the Lord. We spent hours as children talking about the serious affairs of life. We were both very responsible, good students; we loved music, but most of all, we enjoyed each other's company. We rejoiced in each other's accomplishments and experienced pain in each other's hurts.

After I had been in seminary for more than a year, I discovered I had many fears about the ministry. The theology I was learning was not all my own by experience. There were members of the seminary community, for instance, who seemed so sure of their relationship with the Lord. They could talk about Him easily as though He were their personal friend. I couldn't speak of Him intimately and began to fear having a church where the people in the congregation knew more than I did about Him. I prayed (an infrequent occurrence in those days) that if He were real in this personal way, He would show me and give me the confidence some of my friends had. In short, I asked Him to give me a Damascus road experience that would be irrefutable. I uttered that silent prayer about a month before John's death while I was attending a homiletics seminar class.

Not too long after we arrived in Ohio, I began to break down and fall apart. I was struck by my own arrogance at thinking I was going to be the comforter and so soon became the one who needed the most comfort. My emotions were raw; I remembered my need to relive President Kennedy's assassination.

Because friends and relatives had to come from great distances, my friend John's funeral was postponed one more day and the torture of waiting now seemed like a nightmare—yet I was compelled to be a part of every moment of it. The viewing was held the night before the funeral and, though the undertakers had done well, his broken body shattered any strength I had left. His wife asked me to touch him and feel the muscles in his arm. In an attempt to comfort her, I did and it tore my heart in two.

I began to feel bitter and alone. No one seemed to realize the deep, dependent friendship we had had and what a loss this was to me. In my loneliness, I began to turn away from all sources of comfort. When my emotions are so raw I tend to retreat into myself and begin to resent anyone trying to pull me out to face some sort of reality known to them but not to me.

Then it was over. Because of my personal suffering, the funeral seemed cold and insensitive. We drove back to Richmond and I was empty. Then I remembered my prayer of the previous month and was beginning to feel God was answering my request by taking John.

This way of thinking is a most cruel deception. It comes from and causes considerable confusion and probably cripples "Christ in us" more haltingly than anything else. I didn't know the Lord well enough then to know that He doesn't answer our prayers by inflicting pain on others—though He will always use these experiences to show us His love. I marvel now that we can be so determined in our deceptions. I have also met many others who are tied in bondage because deep down they believe some prayer of theirs has been the cause of another's suffering or death. How far our confusion can carry us away from our Lord's self-sacrificing love for us! When we pray, we pray to our loving Father. He will only answer our prayers according to His loving kindness and goodness toward us.

Ask, and it will be given you; seek, and you will find; knock, and it will be opened to you. For every one who asks receives, and he who seeks finds, and to him who knocks it will be opened. Or what man of you, if his son asks him for bread, will give him a stone? Or if he asks for a fish, will give him a serpent? If you then, who are evil, know how to give good gifts to your children, how much more will your Father who is in heaven give good things to those who ask him! (*Matt. 7:7-11*)

We pray from our humanity, from His Spirit within us, from our fear and sin, but He will only answer from His great overwhelming and personal love for us. As we grow and mature in Christ, we find more and more of our prayers proceeding from His Spirit within and being answered in a way we expect through faith.

I didn't hate Him, but I didn't understand Him. I was beginning to feel guilty that I had prayed such a prayer and that I had not pursued this relationship with the Lord through an active prayer life, Bible study, etc., instead of needing a Damascus road experience. I was totally convicted that I, like Thomas, had to be shown; that I could not believe enough by the hearing, and that the showing (necessary for me) was causing so much pain. As the impact of this guilt began to grow, it was fed by the thought that my friend John never needed the pulpit to share Jesus. Indeed, he felt he could be a more effective witness as an engineer. I, on the other hand, needed the support and protection of the pulpit to talk about Jesus, life values, my inmost thoughts. If the Lord was going to remove someone—why not me? I was the insincere one. Why John, the honest witness to His love? I was only comforted with the thought that the Lord had greater work in the kingdom for John to do. I was sinking down in my own heart. Guilt began to overwhelm me and I knew I needed to talk to someone. Judy and I went through a whole list of names and in a seminary community there could be many helpful people. But my mind refused them all—save one—because I didn't know what he would say. I had predetermined all the others' answers, and those I had already dismissed. We invited this one to come over and hear my pain on Thanksgiving night. He left his wife at home and came immediately. I explained the whole story, telling him of the unbearable guilt that was now my constant companion, that my seemingly selfish prayer had caused my dear friend's death. The only sense of life I had by now was my heartbeat and breathing. Emotionally, spiritually—in every other way—I was dead. Though I didn't know what he would say, I never expected what he actually said. I remember it clearly—he calmly said, "You *are* guilty." I thought I couldn't die any more but I was to learn there was yet one more death.

My friend left. My mind raced from one escape door to the next and I discovered that none was open. Finally I came to the door where the Lord was and knew instantly that He had died. Jesus died because of my sin. The story really didn't need a Peter to deny, a Judas to betray, a centurion to spear. If none of these had lived, if I were the only person ever to live—still the Son of God would have had to die—my sin was enough for Him to come. (My sin alone was sufficient cause because of His love and who He is. He had allowed me to feel guilty for John's death, in order for me to experience the guilt for His death through a simple transference. Then I experienced the suffering of His death for me. There was no way for my sin to be forgiven except through the death of Jesus.) Now I was totally dead. Each breath was painful and relief was only coming through thoughts of suicide. I remembered Judas and knew now why he had to commit suicide—he could choose nothing else—the sooner the better. Then I walked into the bedroom and lay down on the bed. Strange how we do such mundane things when the world crashes around us and life seems to be gone. I had just lain down when I started to cry uncontrollably. I don't remember asking for forgiveness but the room filled with a brilliant light and I had to shield my eyes with my arm. In an instant He forgave me and loved me. I felt warm; I wept, I rejoiced, I knew a joy I'd never known before. I kept praying, "Thank you, thank you." I loved the Lord even as a young child but now I knew Him as the Savior and Shepherd of my soul, as my real Lord, as the One who truly forgave those who had murdered Him. He answered my prayer; a most important prayer of the previous month not only as He always faithfully does but in the way He knew I needed to hear, using the very tragic circumstances of my friend's death to bring new life.

My zeal could not be quenched. I wrote everyone in my family. I told all my friends and some of my professors. I reread all my study and textbooks of the previous seminary years and for the first time in my remembrance I was thirsting to learn. I couldn't learn enough. I was also becoming unbearable and, as I look back, quite judgmental. I was frightening some people with my zeal while others rejoiced with me in my experience. Since it had happened so dramatically in my life, I believed it was a normative experience for everyone. I was now sure of my Lord in the same way I had seen evidenced in my seminary classmates. I thought all must experience this same kind of forgiveness. Only years later was I to know there are many Christians who confess Jesus as their Lord and Savior, and who receive His forgiveness in faith, without such an experience.

One of the professors I told of my experience mentioned that history records many such witnesses and he referred me to a few of the great ones, then cautioned me in a way I thought strange at the time but now I understand it. He said, "Be careful not to fall into the Savior complex." I remember thinking quite rationally that we had the advantage of seminary training and religious experience—we really should set the world on fire. Our class did have a lot of spirit and by the time we were called out from one another's company and the cloistered halls of theological training, we were prepared, arrogant and a force to reckon with. Another professor taught us to dare to believe what Jesus said and did and to consider our sainthood in God and brotherhood in Jesus. The difficulty is in identifying so closely with Jesus as a Son of God that motives of human pride can unconsciously intermingle with the pure witness of the Spirit within us, demonstrating Jesus. We can embody the truth, easily discern what is false, grow in sonship and power, and ever so subtly live as though we were the Savior. We can forget the Lord works through many people and circumstances to bring another to himself.

Fourteen years later, I am still learning from that experience. All my life I've been a very dependent person. My journey in the Spirit has been particularly and strongly marked by the Lord gently nudging me and sometimes painfully wrenching me away from unhealthy dependencies in order to place all I am in His hands. I've had a continual battle with letting go, giving up, moving out of the Lord's way, being at peace with what He is doing in the lives of others. "What about John, Lord?"

"Let go, Peter, and follow me."

Shortly after my friend's death and after Thanksgiving, 1964, I preached my middler sermon. Not coincidentally, the text was "Peter, do you love me more than these?" I knew Peter's pain and my tears then, as now, were the window to my divided heart; one part vulnerable in my humanity and hanging on to people and experiences, the other firmly placed in the Lord's renewing love.

Within the Spirit, I have learned to pray fervently and constantly. How many times I have surrendered all I am to the Lord. And He takes me at my word.

"Yes, Lord, you know I love you."

"Then follow me. Feed my lambs. Feed. Give. Feed. Don't worry about John. Follow me. If I call one to die or live what concern is that to you? Become transparent and allow my love to flow through you but, once given, let it go."

Now I know what Jesus means, at least in part, when He asks us to give up everything to follow Him, especially the people and things you cherish most—family, friends, gifts, even love. Dependency upon these must clearly flow from and through Him—He must grow in being our first love in order for these to become the deep, free, radical loving commitments He intends for them to be.

I also know what Paul meant, at least in part, when he said he became all things to all people, that he was transparent enough to do so and further that he was able to glory alone in the cross of Christ. Grace is sufficient. We walk alone to the cross. We cannot say, "Come with me, Jane, Dick, Mary. Take my hand while I go to the cross." We must go alone. So must all those we love. We cannot hang on or say, "Don't go." We can truly only be a praise and glory to God through our simple yes to Him. "Lord, you know I love you" must become "Lord, I love you."

In the meantime, how do we deal with our humanity? I can only say how the Lord deals with me. He shows me the cost; He shows me the potential damage I may create when I love out of my need, my humanity. To honestly face this, He shows me the protection of

His grace for others when I approach them through my own feelings or my need to hang on; He shows me the danger and explosiveness of love not totally grounded in Him; He shows me the pain and burden of people too dependent on me and not enough on Him; He shows me the emptiness of no feelings, emotions or gifts of the Spirit—all of which I had become again too dependent upon; He shows me the hypocrisy and emptiness of moving a mountain without priorities of love. He shows me the need to heal my own humanity. Curiously, I have discovered that this doesn't mean to sanctify or spiritualize my humanity before I have had a chance to recognize it for what it is and honestly admit my daily human need for deliverance. Layer upon layer must be lovingly stripped back toward the need to depend only upon Him. Paradoxically, I must grasp only very lightly anything He has given me, while radically committing myself toward the same because it is His call. I cannot follow the course of another even though it may be and often is identical. I must follow Him alone, and out of this, weld myself totally to those whom He has given me to love. And again He shows me that my trust and love must go toward Him. I must grow in this daily and therefore I cannot hold on to past experiences of His love. Fourteen years ago I experienced Jesus as my Savior in a deeper certainty than I'd ever known. As I grew in dependence upon Him from that time, I learned a continuing salvation. It was not only my own but it was the way He saves others—removing our pride continuously from us. We do not save—He does. I was still to learn His lordship in my life and it didn't come until several more years had passed and I was ready to receive a new experience of His Holy Spirit.

O Lord Jesus, I thank you and praise you for your salvation in my life and in the lives of those you have given me to love and who have loved me with such faithfulness. I thank you for your obedience even in the cross and for your faithfulness to forgive even the most grievous sinner. And I thank you for your patient and gentle love which you have so willingly shown me when I've asked and have so graciously surrounded me with when I've not asked. I thank you for childhood friends and friends today who have become the body of Christ for us now in our lives. Amen.

3

Encounter with Satan— Baptism of Fire and Jesus, My Victorious Lord

To that end keep alert with all perseverance, making supplication for all the saints, and also for me, that utterance may be given me in opening my mouth boldly to proclaim the mystery of the gospel, for which I am an ambassador in chains; that I may declare it boldly, as I ought to speak. (Eph. 6:18-20)

The call came late into the night which was not unusual in our Providence inner-city ministry. We had been conditioned in the first years of our residence as the family of the manse in the Smith Hill neighborhood of Providence to expect to deal with problems and situations foreign to our otherwise innocent and "secure" suburban backgrounds. I had already grown to appreciate, on the positive side, the rawness of truth among so many of the people who live in the heart of the city and attend church there. They did not attempt to cover up who they were nor the wrongdoings they were involved in as their more sophisticated suburban counterparts often do. It was refreshing to work with people who wore few masks, who were ready to dig in and commit themselves to problem solving. Alternatively, however, people in the crowded, congested city also live in and around a more violent, extreme life style and their problems, though up front and honestly admitted, are deep and complicated with a series of related problems that are often accepted as normal living. It is not uncommon to find persons alone with long-term alcoholic sicknesses, violent temperaments, long arrest records, and venereal diseases while being unemployed, uneducated, and sleeping in cars—all wrapped up in one body and who look for help out of sheer desperation.

But the Lord has given us hope and, banded together in unity, that hope is undaunted. For me, this hope and positive approach was to receive its severest battering in a contest I was totally unprepared for.

The phone conversation had lasted for two hours. The young woman on the other end, age twenty-six, mother of one daughter, raised in a Christian home, spoke coherently of her attempted suicide just hours before. I had never received a hotline call like this before. I experienced total frustration and growing hopelessness as we talked. She had recited a long list of sins to which I responded with the Lord's forgiveness. He had gifted me somewhere very early in my life with the vision to see through the sin to the hurt in a person and, if I put my mind to it, I could always find His forgiveness—never His condemnation. There have been times when my heart could not or did not follow through and I would hold grudges and resentments—but I always knew better. Furthermore, I was always aware of my own sin, always knew or believed in His forgiveness for me, and never felt my sin was any less than that of the worst sinner. The sin of the inward heart in its faithlessness is as grave as any outward demonstration.

She told me in a later conversation that it was this attitude of forgiveness that led her to talk to me again the next day. I had also discovered at a later point that she had called a good friend of mine also in the ministry just minutes before her first call to me and she hung up the phone when he, more wisely, but perhaps less delicately, set the ground rules of further conversations and essentially placed the decision of life or death back upon her. She was apparently unwilling for that to happen then (although I ultimately came to this point much later and she was still unwilling) and—the Lord was surely dealing with me.

Her problems, at least the ones she told me that night, involved alcohol, heroin addiction, prostitution, all intertwined with organized crime. My basic reaction centered in the Lord's love for her and that she still had much to live for. I knew it would be a long program of restoration. The more I tried to convince her, however, the worse things became. I remember thinking that finally we would talk about her daughter and that that would bring a sense of purpose to her future. She did indeed love her daughter and did desire a good life for her. Ironically, it was for this reason she had attempted suicide; during the week previously she had, in an uncontrolled fit of passion, tried to kill her daughter. Though the guilt was deep and she could accept forgiveness for even this—the fear was deeper that it might happen again and, therefore, she felt her daughter would be better off without her.

Everything I proposed that might engender some spark of hope was met by a mind determined to destroy itself; the wall seemed impenetrable. The next day she came with her girl friend and their daughters (her friend also lived in a similar malevolent maze of existence) to talk further and it seemed to take us down roads that led nowhere. In the late afternoon I offered to take them home and Barbara, who had called me the night before, jumped at the chance. I discovered later that she was to meet the man who would provide her with the heroin she needed for the day. So she was already very nervous as we started for her home.

We weren't there too long before we all discovered he was not going to make the connection. This provided the first real opening to work on something positive. I decided I would stay if she would go through withdrawal. She lived with her friend who asked me to stay because she was frightened to meet this alone. Much to our surprise, Barbara agreed and we settled in for the hours of anguish and pain. I left around 3:00 A.M.—the worst was over but I was beginning to feel I was in over my head and needed help. Now that a step toward rehabilitation had been taken, I felt that the whole situation was even more delicate than before. I was critically aware of the fact that no mistakes could be made at this point lest more harmful complications might develop.

The next day I called Fr. John Randall of St. Patrick's Parish for help and this became the first open acknowledgment on my part that I needed something I knew he had. Our relationship had been friendly up to this point; we had been mutually supportive of one another's work and we liked one another instantly. So now I must turn to another thread in the story before going on to Barbara.

Fr. Randall was the impetus for the Catholic charismatic movement in Rhode Island with its particular roots in the Holy Ghost Parish of Federal Hill in Providence. The prayer group that developed became known as the Word of God Community and moved into St. Patrick's Parish in Smith Hill. The entire story of how the Holy Spirit moved through Fr. Randall from the very beginning days when he was one of the spiritual advisors to Ralph Martin and Steve Clark (and who, incidentally, advised them in 1967 to leave this whole experience alone) to 1975 can be found in his book *In God's Providence.* At the time I made my phone call to him he had become an internationally known leader in the renewal, remaining firmly entrenched in Smith Hill and what the Lord was doing here.

The objective of the Word of God Community in Providence had become, through the offices of then Bishop McVinney, the renewal of a dying parish. It was under the leadership of a seven-person pastoral team headed by Fr. Randall and Fr. Raymond Kelly. They were assigned to St. Patrick's Parish in Smith Hill which, though several times larger, was experiencing the same urban blight and death as the church I was serving. Judy and I had come to Providence in December, 1968, and were firmly entrenched in our work with the church and community when the summer of 1971 came around and the Word of God Community took up residence in and around St. Patrick's about one-half mile from our church and home.

Judy developed a first-hand knowledge of what was happening very early. She started attending prayer meetings as early as the fall of 1971, went through the Life in the Spirit seminars, received the baptism of the Holy Spirit, employed the gifts of the Spirit and prayed for me—all of which escaped most of my notice since I was so heavily involved in other directions. She had invited me to the prayer meetings. I did attend two and was impressed with the love and joy that were overwhelmingly evident but which, ironically, helped turn me even more staunchly toward a seriousness in Christianity which found its mark in all of our work with the poor, moving continually toward a deeper justice in social-civil life. Many of my friends in community work were becoming attracted to the love of the Spirit, and I tried to listen graciously to their stories while experiencing mixed emotions inside—a happiness for them but also a resentment and frustration that their commitments in our work together were being altered. In some instances, I was having to shoulder even more responsibility because of their new directions, and my pride was being pricked.

For some months previously, the pastors of two American Baptist churches and I had met weekly to share and, in time, plan the full cooperative union of our churches again in the neighborhood—the one being a block away. We thought it good to expand our discussions and fellowship and, by mutual agreement with Father Randall, we began to meet. Our intentions were to find even more avenues for cooperative work. Father Randall began teaching the Life in the Spirit seminar. I didn't last long in the seminar because I considered other commitments to be more pressing. The two Baptist pastors continued to the end. The three of us also continued to meet. And all three of us somehow managed to escape involvement in the renewal. On the other hand, we did not escape a brush with one of the Lord's servants whom He intended to use in a deeply loving and majestic way in my life many months later.

I did not campaign against the charismatic renewal and don't remember speaking against it but did often think and say that it was a radical answer for radical problems, that it was observably a very loving and joyful movement, that it was perhaps meant for many but not all and certainly not for me. I remember being critical of some prayers I heard; they seemed selfish and not very austere. I would always see first the hurt it could cause others if they were answered the way people expected. I needed to learn that the Father does indeed desire to bless His children and would never do so by hurting another. (The hurt we often feel stems from our own envy and pride.) I remember also feeling a subtle put-down on the part of some, for they would say such things as "Some day it will happen to you," "I will continue to pray for you"; all as if they were saying, "I know something you don't know—I have something you don't have." I shared this burden with Judy (I did not see that my pride was being hurt) and she in her love for me stopped going to prayer meetings and other activities surrounding the renewal. But she didn't stop praying!

About a month before Barbara called I remember two things happening to prepare the way. I was beginning to feel the need to more effectively pastor the people in the church and, though this never formed itself into an audible prayer, it was in my heart. The first step I took toward this direction was to give up Johnny Carson and use that late-night time for disciplined intercessory prayer for the people in the church. It was a good time, usually uninterrupted, and really the only available time during the day. I also remember a time of sharing with Robert Fitzgerald, proprietor of the Earthen Vessel, a used-clothing store in Smith Hill dedicated to the Lord's poor. Bob had talked to me many times about the renewal and witnessed to what the Lord had done in his life. I didn't know until later that the Lord had really given him a burden for me and with a great sense of mission, he would find every opportunity to bend my ear. Again, however, pride was not allowing my heart to bend and I found myself walking other streets to avoid the storefront Earthen Vessel. As the Lord would have it, however, I remember clearly a beautiful balmy day in September, a festival day, when spirits were high. For perhaps three solid hours I was with Bob; he did most of the talking, and I was becoming in full agreement with things I had rejected from his lips before and I was getting more and more excited as he went on. I discovered later that he also talked with Judy and told her he thought something was happening inside me. She understood what he meant but it was still months later when she could finally share with me about that festival day when I too could understand. All I knew then was that it seemed to be an unusual day—a day that baffled even me because I was no longer resisting—even though it was only then I realized I had been resisting. I even knew that Judy and others had prayed for a beautiful, balmy day and it didn't bother me that they had or that it was such a day—and I didn't think once of the farmers who might have been hurt by the weather because they needed rain. Indeed, they must have also prayed for the Lord to work wonders on this day—for so He did.

I told Barbara I would get back to her the next day to see how she was doing. I didn't until I called Father Jake Randall. I knew they had ministered deeply to persons with heavy drug addictions and that the radical nature of their ministry (baptism of the Holy Spirit) had provided a permanent cure even in very hard-core cases. I needed their help. Jake sensed I needed more than advice. He told me he would be available any time to help. He assigned Miss Jean Zibilski to me who was familiar with these kinds of problems and who was free to help me at that time. I didn't realize then the magnitude of the help or love this involved; nor did I envision the days ahead and the sacrifices Judy would have to make, for I was beginning to be consumed by this situation. I know that for at least a month I slept no more than two or three hours a night, yet I felt refreshed when I woke up. Only the Lord knows how much love and time were poured out by all the others involved in what was to become a consuming fire.

I called Barbara and offered the help I was receiving. It would be necessary for movement toward life that had begun the night before because I couldn't handle what was needed alone. Barbara and her friend were both afraid but said they would call me back. They trusted me but they weren't sure of others. I assured them they could trust anyone I brought, for we would all respect their confidence.

They called back that evening at the church where we were co-sponsoring a fellowship night with the Baptist church around the corner. The evening's program was a magic show for children. While planning the event seemed innocuous enough, by the time the evening actually came, Barbara's call was expected, people were in grave trouble, and Jake and others stood ready to pour out their lives in love for the Lord. Both Judy and I felt the rumblings of something much larger and more fearful than a magician plying his tricks. We could not tell anyone what was happening and why we could not laugh. I often reflect upon loneliness at such times—for all people—but especially pastors and their wives, priests and healers who are the Lord's chosen shepherds, who are frail and bruised just as any other, yet try so hard to answer the call of His love and joy and hope. Sheep can so easily misunderstand

and be hurt.

Barbara called to say she agreed to my offer of additional help, and Jean and I went down late that night to her home. I acquainted Jean with all that had happened. We prayed. Judy was praying at home. I know people were set in intercessory prayer at St. Patrick's. Significantly, Jean asked Barbara and her friend that evening if they ever had anything to do with the occult.

"Yes."

"How much?" They could not say. I remember laughing at the suggestion Satan was real—but enough for this night. On the way home Jean filled me in a little on their experience with people in the occult and my laughter ended. Now I knew I would have to deal with my theological training which placed Satan neatly and comfortably in a first-century thought-form. Somehow he was emerging into the sophisticated twentieth century and my mind was whirling like a computer.

Judy, Jake and Jean immediately felt there was need for additional help. My fears were beginning to show. Sister Fran Conway, a person filled with the Lord's love who had been involved since the very beginning days of renewal in Federal Hill, was to accompany us on our next trip to Barbara's home—two days later. Again, before we could go, bridges of trust needed to be built and by this time Barbara and her friend were afraid too.

This next visit, now five days after the first phone call, was to be a time of the Lord's revelation—a revelation so powerful that it would make any heart cry out, "My Lord and my God."

I remember a slide of the U.S. Army in Korea. It was projected on a screen sometime during our time in Hagerstown. The man showing the slide was a veteran of that conflict. It pictured a number of U.S. Army officers standing on a hillside above a row of several howitzers. Standing with the officers, who were all wearing sophisticated sunglasses, were their South Korean counterparts. The explanation of the slide was that on this day there had been a demonstration of U.S. air and field fire power for the Koreans and this was one section of artillery in the demonstration.

This same night I witnessed the fire power of Satan and my Lord Jesus Christ and am thrilled to report that our Lord Jesus was the victor. I saw evil more subtle and disgusting than armies and bombs and love more powerful and victorious than all the evil Satan can muster. I came away knowing that Satan lived and was as much of a person as you and I. I possessed a hatred for him like none other.

That evening we discovered that Barbara and her friend had taken a nine-year blood pact with Satan that they would serve him in any way he chose. They were witches in that service, and had already witnessed a human sacrifice. They had cursed each other and, before us even then, tried to kill themselves and were powerless to resist. I was speechless but I tried to help where I could. The mention of Jesus' name caused Barbara to go into a trance several times and apparently lose the ability to hear. The Lord spoke through Sisters Fran and Jean directly to their souls and only Jesus in the mystery of His love was able to turn their hearts toward Him.

The story goes on even to this day but, suffice it to say, the Lord continues to work out His loving purpose and victory in Barbara's life, the life of her friend, and their two daughters. Many things have resulted from these beginnings; it was the start of a long and beautiful journey.

There was, for instance, the immediate need for yet more help and we met and grew to love very deeply three other people—Matt Tierney, then the person in the St. Patrick's pastoral team who led their ministries of physical healing, deliverance and inner healing, and Ladd and June Fields who were on loan in apostolic ministry from the Redeemer Episcopal Church of Houston, Texas. Through hundreds of meetings and chance conversations, we all grew dependent upon one another as true brothers and sisters in the same family.

Because of the involvements in Barbara's life there was an opportunity to witness to the Attorney General of Rhode Island and a member of his staff.

The effect upon my ministry in the United Presbyterian Church was immediate. It took shape primarily in the pastorate but also had positive influences in the Providence Presbytery and the 1976 General Assembly in Baltimore.

The impetus toward unity in the Christian family that began here is still having effects that defy measurement but which I believe have profound and historic significance.

The revelations to self, the convictions of the Holy Spirit in my life, the continuing transformation of my personality and humanity brought about some dramatic changes.

The love which Judy and I were given by the Lord for each other grew in great leaps over the pains and hurts that are normal when a deep relationship is brought toward greater oneness.

My understanding of the Word of God came alive and for the first time I could begin to accept mysteries, paradoxes, and truths for what they were without having to bend them to fit the need for a consistent theology in my analytical mind.

Not the least new theological understanding was the knowledge—the "knowing" confirmed in life experience—that when the Word speaks of a personal, powerful, vile and evil enemy called Satan and when it describes his work, when it warns the children of God to be aware of the nature and continual struggle of warfare against us—it means exactly and precisely what it says! I've seen demons fall, Satan recede and souls snatched from the fiery pit of hell with one word, the Word—spoken boldly with great authority or even softly and gently. JESUS!

O Lord, how great thou art. My Lord, my God—I fall before your love for us all—a love so deep and penetrating, a love so personal and affectionate, a love so paradoxical and mysterious, a love so far beyond our understanding, yet as close and well known as the next breath we breathe.

Father, thank you for your promised Holy Spirit, and His empowering life within us. Thank you for showing us in the firmness and gentleness of a Father's love the enemy who is set against us. Thank you, Lord Jesus, for your obedience to the cross, your faithful light in the darkness of hell and your resurrection day. Thank you, Jesus, for your victory, for the dayspring and morning star, for the Lion of Judah and the strong arm that goes before us. Thank you for walking with us in the valley as well as on the plain and up the mountain side.

Father, I ask in Jesus' name, that you would end the confusion and deception among your children once and for all and show them the nature of the enemy who seeks to devour us. Draw us together, one victorious body, to the glory of Jesus Christ. Amen.

4

Giving of Gifts—Discovery of Sonship and God, My Father

And because you are sons, God has sent the Spirit of his Son into our hearts, crying, "Abba! Father!" So through God you are no longer a slave but a son, and if a son then an heir. (Gal. 4:6-7)

The world changed and, as if transported by some time machine, we began to live in the first century. Unlike many people who experience the baptism of the Holy Spirit (or what I now prefer to think of as a releasing of the power of the Holy Spirit already resident within us, or even more generally, a deepening experience of the Lord), our growth in the Spirit seemed to be slow, constant and steady as opposed to the ups and downs or spiritual highs and lows so often evident in the charismatic renewal. Our ascent up the mountain of life in the Spirit became a fairly steady climb but, as I see it now, without needed rest periods.

We started moving toward the timberline with our first and perhaps most significant lesson from the Word of God. Jesus now meant everything to us and we recognized Him as the baptizer and one who filled us with the power of the Holy Spirit. Though we knew Him as our Savior and now recognized Him ever more fully each day as our Lord, Jesus was also our brother and friend. The significance of this was not easy to grasp nor was it quick in coming.

Much time had been spent in learning from Matt Tierney the many facets of spiritual warfare. We went through deliverance ourselves and read the scores of books published concerning the renewal. We bought all the records of renewal music we could find and played them each day. We attended prayer meetings by the dozens, and shared on numerous occasions with Ladd and June Fields about their experiences with the Lord in Redeemer Church. Then we settled in for a time of teaching that Ladd would give not only for us but for our church. The theme of his teaching was simple and basic but it became for many a real stumbling block. He taught us from the Word what it meant that God had placed His seed of righteousness within us and that we were, because of His action, saints. We had all somehow been trained to see ourselves almost exclusively as sinners and as much as we knew our salvation was by grace and by His first act of love toward us, we still found ourselves striving and anxious, quite unlike the lilies of the field, driven toward earning our righteousness and sainthood. I'm not saying we didn't know this was wrong but deep within us there is a false sense of unworthiness (inverted pride) instead of a healthy sense of humility which recognizes paradoxically that we are indeed unworthy to even be in the presence of Jesus while conversely we share full life with Him as our brother. We are sons of God, joint heirs of the kingdom, raised by the same Father, full of power and authority. He has already forgiven us (if we repent) but we negate so much of that forgiveness and its great healing power by withholding forgiveness from ourselves. Since our pride is usually so great, we are afraid of loving ourselves. Since we can often condemn ourselves so easily, nothing on earth can budge our hearts open for our own love to flow toward ourselves. We know the record—we've been forgiven and we are loved by God, our Father, especially through Jesus but we spend the rest of our lives being set free by that love—first to love ourselves and then to love others. Satan has a proverbial heyday keeping us locked up in our own bondage, causing us to acquiesce to his suggestions and live passively instead of boldly for and with Jesus. This causes us to grumble and be anxious when we ought to always place upon our sleeves joyful hearts, rejoicing that our names are written in the Lamb's Book of Life. Furthermore, he causes us to be concerned with trivia, keeping us confused about ourselves and our place in the body of Christ instead of dealing with the movement of the Spirit as confirmed sons of God.

Ladd continued to hammer away at the truth and some of us fully recognized we were learning from a genuine apostle as much as if we were sitting in the living rooms of Peter or James or John. We picked up a sense of adventure and vision. We began to picture ourselves walking the streets of Smith Hill as Paul walked the streets of Ephesus or Peter walked the streets of Jerusalem, offering, in power and grace, our Lord Jesus to any who would simply stretch forth a hand. Nothing was impossible and out of that sense grew a vision of a loving, healing community that would be the light of the world. So high would Jesus be lifted up in our praise that the heavens would even take notice. We were the sons of God, called to bestride the world like Colossus. How many times we wept warm tears of joy in those days when our hearts were hearts of flesh, touched at the least little victory of the Spirit. Our vision was to see every business, home and street, each family, institution and structure transformed into His likeness. We asked for every gift and believed it was given to us.

It was a long time before I received the gift of tongues but the night I did half a dozen of us were gathered in our living room in prayer around our coffee table. At the moment of the first utterance a stack of newspapers in our basement fell over with a crash—a gate of the Spirit had been opened. Judy's first prayer in tongues years before was a word she did not know then (even though she had helped me all through seminary with my Greek vocabulary and other biblical languages) and a word we were all to learn in deep appreciation—"Abba"! When she first uttered this word, not knowing its meaning, uncontrollable tears flowed from her eyes. The prayer language the Lord has given me has never been something I've understood, but as I grew in the use of prayer in tongues and found it to be my constant companion, I discovered two things happening. First, through the use of this way of praying the Lord would provide words of knowledge especially when praying for another person's healing. Secondly, after at least 10,000 words (I found this length easier and easier to achieve as I fell into a discipline of praying while walking, especially along the streets of the Hill), a conscious prayer, short and concise, would form and I knew those prayers came from the Spirit and, when I uttered them, things were accomplished as He saw fit. Early in our trek up the mountain, we had learned of the volatile nature of this gift and never used it as confirmation of the baptism in the Spirit. While we encouraged it because of its own beauty and God-given nature, we never allowed it to become a stumbling block. We heard Catherine Marshall LeSourd speak at the Fourth International Presbyterian Conference on the Holy Spirit in Montreat, North Carolina, and took her advice as our own. Concerning tongues, the baptism or anything else of the Spirit, it is best to simply encourage anyone who has problems with these things to ask the Lord, "Is there something more and do you have something more for me?" This places the situation properly where it belongs—between the Christian and his Lord, dealing with that particular Christian's faith, at his level. I wish I had learned this wisdom as easily in other situations because when I didn't I found myself presuming upon the Lord.

One such instance of this presumption became clear to me only after some damage had been sustained on the part of people in the congregation. Because of my experience with Satan and because I had come out of a twentieth-century world view of evil which has depersonalized and demythologized biblical concepts of evil (and sin), I felt it was necessary for the people of the congregation to accept this new awareness even if they had to open themselves to similar experiences. Though I still believe Christians need to be aware of the reality of Satan and his methods, and this is particularly important today, I now recognize it is not only an alien concept that violates most people's thinking but it is also particularly frightening to most of us. When I was pushing so hard for this awareness among the people in the congregation, I was doing so out of many demonstrable fears of my own as well as my knowledge of the truth. At that time I was still actively dealing with Barbara and her friend, and many times I had to talk not to Barbara and her friend but to Satan through them; I prayed "Jesus" while Satan spewed out his vile incantations against Christians. I admit there were times when I was afraid and I'm sure I passed on this fear. I did not find balance right away because I decided to speak only of Jesus' victory, love and healing. Consequently, I began to lose some of my own awareness of the enemy or at least to let it lie dormant. I grew to laugh at Satan and think of him as nothing. It was only during times when we would minister deliverance that I would be reminded again of my own experience; that I would, for a time, be on guard, while in the meantime I would watch confusions and half-truths grow, forgetting their source. After all this and the hurt that grew out of it, I remembered the advice we heard concerning tongues and was able to apply the same in terms of knowledge of the enemy. It is just as presumptuous to demand that people become aware as it is not to speak the full truth. Robert E. Lee was one of my boyhood idols and I remember learning somewhere back on the pages of early reading that one of the most significant contributing factors to his incredible battlefield successes was his knowledge of the enemy. He knew the Potomac armies as well as he knew his own and was always one step ahead of them. There is no substitute for knowing your enemy. In our case as Christians, Paul makes it clear who our enemy really is but I've discovered Jesus is our best teacher and He desires for us to learn, wherever possible, in the classroom of the Word where hearts are lovingly open to Him rather than on the fearful battlefield for the first time. We will go to the battlefield sure enough but our equipment for the battle will have been hewn in the factories of our homes and churches—by His Word. Then we won't need to presume the strategy of battle when we arrive on the field. One Commander in our army is enough.

The gift of hope was always there but now it was accompanied by stronger faith. We now had power to believe and one Scripture after another took on deeper meaning. The Lord was now with us when two or three were gathered in His name so we knew His continual presence both in ourselves and in community. The vision He gave us became real and unseen things became as bread at every meal. Our vision is perhaps not unlike that of many communities who sense the Lord's powerful moving Spirit. We believed in, and still do believe in, a community with so much prayer power and praise that is so inwardly and visually peaceful, so deeply loving and Christ-centered, that a visitor might only walk through or drive on our streets and, perhaps without even realizing what had happened, receive healing of whatever kind the Lord desired to give. Our prayer is that vistors might so clearly perceive Him that their hearts would be opened upon just approaching the borders of our neighborhood. There is one essential ingredient in the vision the Lord gave that a few of us believe with all our hearts—*it will only happen if we are one!*

Two Scriptures became our watchword: "Then they said to him, 'What must we do, to be doing the works of God?' Jesus answered them, 'This is the work of God, that you believe in him whom He has sent' " (John 6:28-29); " 'I do not pray for these only, but also for those who believe in me through their word, that they may all be one; even as thou, Father, art in me, and I in thee, that they also may be in us, so that the world may believe that thou hast sent me' " (John 17:20-21). How is the world to know about Jesus' saving love? How is it to be evangelized? The most serious answer lies in these verses and so the Lord gave us vision and hope in our community—a place where it could actually happen—a real city set upon the hill with light to shine the world over. More about this later.

Peace—a hard gift for me, fraught with perhaps more struggle than any other. The Lord has given me peace or let me struggle to find it in Him so many times that I share the lesson He has taught me over and over again. I must learn to let go. With my sins of presumption, anxiety over things beyond my control, driving desire for people to know and receive certain things concerning Him, worry and concern over some individuals I know He loves yet who do not open up to the fullness of that love—all coupled with my own emotional insecurities and needs to place people in a dependent role upon me, and my pride which needs to be victorious in problem-solving and ahead of others' efforts—have all worked together to make me unpeaceful in many situations and therefore in great need of His loving peace. I would often carry burdens of crushing weight or bear responsibility that wasn't even mine, all to the detriment of the ministry. On the other hand, I've always known the peace of the gift of eternal life and of His loving kindness. Certain Scriptures have brought comfort though I'm still learning their meaning—"Consider the lilies . . . they neither toil nor spin yet I tell you, even Solomon in all his glory was not arrayed like one of these" (Matt. 6:28-29); "My yoke is easy, and my burden is light" (Matt. 11:30); "Do not be anxious about tomorrow . . . let the day's own trouble be sufficient for the day" (Matt. 6:34). Peace would and did come in many situations and I discovered my peace brought an end to some significant hostilities and divisions especially in the church and for a time we seemed to grow unhindered. I also discovered, however, that before long others were willing to carry the burden of anxiety and we went back to first base.

Gifts of healing were being given to many in our church body and while some refused to receive them for various reasons, others did not. In spite of this giving of gifts and the fact we never really coordinated or structured a healing ministry, the Lord would continue to astound us by healing someone we didn't pray for or even know how to pray for.

Since few fully recognized the evidence of demonic activity among and in Christians in the church, our ministry dealing with this was limited and cautious. Deliverance of spirits in church and in homes was done very quietly and so unobtrusively that only the few of us who were involved in this ministry were aware of it. The Lord would continue to give us knowledge, however, and in faith we proceeded with that knowledge of specific demonic and spirit activity often as we gathered for Sunday worship or more openly in prayer meetings. There were a handful of instances where times were scheduled for individual ministry in deliverance when people requested this help. In prayer and fasting and simple faith we would follow step by step the Lord's guidance. It was common for us to witness His powerful deliverance.

Inner healing prayers were often said. It was not uncommon to be led by the Spirit in pastoral prayer during worship or more informal prayer at our weekly prayer meetings in the gentle healing of the inner man by Jesus.

Various other gifts and manifestations of the Spirit were evident from time to time in the form of visions, prophecies, words of knowledge, hearing the wind of the Spirit in an otherwise calm setting or smelling the sweet fragrance of perfume in unlikely places.

As our understanding of healing increased and we began to open ourselves up to be instruments of the Lord's healing, many beautiful things happened. Relationships found sufficient grace for exposing and healing wounds of longstanding. Emotionally unstable, spiritually immature or volatile personalities were experiencing inner growth and healing.

One experience of healing will remain my teacher for a long time. Though Jane's healing affected the church in many ways, I will only write here about the ways in which God used this gift to help me. I had made an appointment to visit Jane in her home, for she had been confined there for some time convalescing from various treatments for a back condition. Jane and her husband, Jim, had joined the church some months earlier and had shared with all of us an unusual degree of faith. Shortly after joining, Jane, who was young and active, was stricken with severe back trouble and in a short time she became severely weakened and finally bedridden. Though discs in her back were disintegrating and an operation was the last alternative, we prayed in previous visits for the Lord to heal her and envisioned Jane walking and running about normally and actively. Her condition had worsened but her faith was continually strengthened to the degree that during this period of time she was especially used by the Lord to strengthen many others. She had worked through any potential resentments she may have had and was filled with deep praise toward the Lord and sincere thanksgiving for the many beautiful gifts He had given her.

While driving to another appointment earlier on the day I was to see Jane, the Lord spoke clearly to me that this was the day and time He desired to bring about the healing we had all prayed for. Somewhat apprehensive, I prayed further, decided to fast the rest of the day, and actively seek the Lord's intentions. I remembered the Scripture of Jesus telling His disciples to cast the net upon the other side of the boat; the Scripture of Jonah being cast into the sea also came to mind. I connected the two and pictured us casting our faith upon the water. In other words, we were to exercise more faith than ever before and, in boldness, proclaim the victory of God's living Word.

As I arrived at Jane's, I announced to her that I felt this was an important day, having already spent most of it preparing for this time together. I felt I was definitely ready. Jane could readily accept the importance of this visit and was willing to pray the whole time rather than simply talk together which we would normally have done. It seemed so momentous and important an occasion to me that the only way we could approach it was through prayer.

Jane was out of traction, which the doctors originally had hoped would forestall the operation, but experienced overwhelming pain while walking and she could not go up and down stairs without becoming exhausted. She was able to sit up in the chair as we began talking but it was obviously painful for her. I told her of what I felt the Lord was saying, shared the Scripture and asked her about all that I had just said. She was immediately one with me in what the Lord was presenting to us, although she was initially apprehensive even as I was. Nevertheless, she prayed quickly and quietly for her own confirmation and the fear quickly passed away. So we decided to open up in prayer to find where the Lord would lead us. First there were some spirits to deal with. Jane quietly cast them out and there were perceptible physical changes. Then there came a simple command-prayer of healing. It was awkward and as I look back on it, I realize it was not very theologically correct but it is what the Lord wanted. It was the first time I ever prayed with anyone this way and I was shaking in my new-found power and realization in prayer. It was, however, the prayer that the Spirit had formed. The Father answered immediately. Jane got up from her chair and for the first time in months felt no pain while she walked. Ironically, I next heard the Lord direct in prayer that I should ask for the ability to "rest in the Spirit" for Jane. I said in my mind, "No, Lord. Jane's back—she could fall." I had just prayed with more faith than I ever had before. I believed her back had been healed. Without asking, she had gotten up and walked joyfully, proclaiming no pain. I knew in my spirit she was healed and thanked the Father right there but when He then asked for this next prayer, I immediately did not believe and thought her back would be damaged if she fell to the floor. It was the same as the Israelites whom He delivered from the mighty armies of Egypt through the parting of the Red Sea—a tremendous series of miracles to deliver His people. Two days later, they lacked faith to believe he would provide food.

My humanity was showing but so was the Lord's sense of humor. I began walking with Jane, again with my human concern that she was weak and didn't need to fall. Just then she fell to the floor peacefully enough, and I knew immediately that she was resting in the Spirit. I laughed, then prayed and many minutes later when she got up we shared together the wonder of our Father who had kept His promise to set her free and heal her. Such a joyful day this was but it was also one which taught me things I didn't want to learn. No matter how spiritual we become, how close and one with God we are, no matter how much faith we exercise, we do not lose our humanity and our deep sense of pride. I never had employed such faith as this, was never more submissive to the Lord (I was so fearful of being otherwise since He had indicated such a dramatic healing) and had done all I knew how to be a pure vessel of His love and healing. Yet many months later I was to come up short one day and realize even in this most joyful experience of the Lord, I had seen something else. In the command-healing prayer He led me to pray, I also saw, upon deeper scrutiny, Adamic sin deep within me, which told the Lord what to do rather than simply glorying in Him. The next chapter deals much more with these convictions of the deep inner man so let me turn here to one other gift that can only really be observed, not claimed.

I have always been aware of a deep-rooted pride in myself and although the Lord nurtures us, and we give up the outward appearance of pride, I never lost track of the fact that deep within me there still lurked a reservoir of unadulterated pride. Shortly after the experience of receiving the power of the Spirit I began to think the Lord had taken away my pride until quite comically one day in a fit of seldom-expressed anger, I pounded my fist on the table and knocked over a coffee cup. The Lord must have known what I needed because the display was so ridiculous that I finally laughed, knowing beyond the shadow of a doubt that He had not taken away my pride—indeed, He had not gifted me with overwhelming humility, and I would spend all my days placing my pride in submission to His Holy Spirit. At any rate, I began to appreciate examples of humility around me. Jesus told the rich young ruler who kept all the commandments and was truly a good man, "There is one thing left you must do," and I believe that the one thing was that he must humble himself before God. Some years ago a good friend was sharing about the Lord in the living room of another friend to a small number of husbands and wives. After the meeting was over, I went up to him and said, "The Lord in you is so beautiful." He smiled a big grin, his eyes filled and he said, "Thank you."

A dear friend, Ron Scopel, who inadvertently taught us many of the principles of the Spirit and much of the love of Jesus by his own example, shared with me an experience he had while in prayer. Ron has always enjoyed a time of peaceful quiet with the Lord in some setting of nature. He is a state social worker in a federal housing project and the burdens of his work are numerous. The simple, prayerful life he leads has been a joy for all of us to witness. He shared with me one particular series of events that began as he went to his prayer place after work one day. He moved toward a hillside which overlooked the entire city of Providence through the trees below. He had noticed as he drove his pickup truck into the area that a dump was behind the hill but the magnificent beauty of the trees and view continued to lead him and he decided to stay there and pray. As he prayed he was struck by the prayer that the Spirit led within him as he asked the Lord to allow him to see His mercy seat. He opened his eyes and his gaze was directed not ahead to the breathtaking view of the entire city but backward toward the dump. His vision focused in upon a dilapidated old stuffed chair with springs sticking out, its arms and legs loose and bent. He asked the Lord if that was His mercy seat. Then he opened the Bible and read these words,

Then you shall make a mercy seat of pure gold; two cubits and a half shall be its length, and a cubit and a half its breadth. And you shall make two cherubim of gold; of hammered work shall you make

them, on the two ends of the mercy seat. Make one cherub on the one end, and one cherub on the other end; of one piece with the mercy seat shall you make the cherubim on its two ends. The cherubim shall spread out their wings above, overshadowing the mercy seat with their wings, their faces one to another; toward the mercy seat shall the faces of the cherubim be. And you shall put the mercy seat on the top of the ark; and in the ark you shall put the testimony that I shall give you. There I will meet with you, and from above the mercy seat, from between the two cherubim that are upon the ark of the testimony, I will speak with you of all that I will give you in commandment for the people of Israel. (Exod. 25:17-22)

So overwhelmed that the Lord was showing him this, Ron asked for a confirming word, opened the Bible again and his eyes fell upon these words:

Let us then with confidence draw near to the throne of grace, that we may receive mercy and find grace to help in time of need. (Heb. 4:16)

Ron went over to the chair in the dump, knelt before it and wept. After a time, he stood up and picked up the chair, moving it into a thicket of trees where it could not be seen. For two weeks he came back every day, knelt and wept before "the mercy seat of God." Then, because of work, he was unable to return to the summit of the hill to pray. The next time he could go he was excited. As he approached the thicket of trees, however, the chair was gone. He looked all around the dump. The chair had not been moved—it was gone.

Into the Holy of Holies and the presence of God where once walked the High Priest himself, we can go. It may be on the mountainside, it may be in your living room, it may be at the dump. Wherever it is, it will be holy ground. The seat of mercy may be an ornate, wood-carved chair but it may also be a discarded, dilapidated old stuffed chair because the holy ground upon which it sits is still stained with the blood of the slain Lamb of God. If we carry the marks of Jesus, it will not only be His power and victory to which we cling but also His humiliation and death. As He let go of the power and victory to accomplish the will of the Father, so must we be willing to do. We can move a mountain with our God-given faith, but without the God-given humility of love, we cannot stand on holy ground.

There's a sense in which we bring before the mercy seat of God our full spirituality and our full humanity but not our sin. We come in total humility and helplessness. We come willing just to be in love with Him—stripped of all else. We come happily, with no specific purpose for our own future other than to love Him. We will then go back into the world loving God rather than the things of God, knowing as never before that Jesus' total relationship with His Father was predicated on this love and humility. There was no guile in Him as He shed His blood for all men, no pride at all as He hung on the cross in complete weakness and humiliation before men, no strength or power as He was stripped in hell. His Father loved Him. He brought Him through the veil of all that stands between our Father and us and Jesus became the only pathway upon which we can go to our Father. In the charred forest of our lives burned to the ground, one may look hard enough and find the little green shoot of life beginning all over again—the small seed of righteousness, the tiny grain of mustard seed—a new hidden nature in Christ.

Dear Father, we love you. You know we can but partially understand your overwhelming love for us through your precious and only-begotten Son, Jesus. We only know little ways of thanking you yet you are satisfied if we only love you. What a wonderful Father you are. Thank you for making us your children. Forgive us our foolish ways. Father, Abba, we love you. Amen.

5

A Lesson in Walking on Water

So in the present case I tell you, keep away from these men and let them alone; for if this plan or this undertaking is of men, it will fail; but if it is of God, you will not be able to overthrow them. You might even be found opposing God! (Acts 5:38-39)

Hid in Christ

I had given everything to Him. He was everything to me and although I was aware that much of my life needed transformation, I believed it would take place, for in the mind of Christ, I also believed, there was a purpose and life for me that would glorify Him and lift Him up. I only wanted to serve Him, to bless Him, to be washed and loved by Him, to be directed in all my steps by His Spirit, to grow ever deeper in my sonship and love for my Father. I took to heart the beautiful prayer of St. Francis and desired only to be an instrument of His peace and where there was hatred to bring love, the beautiful love of Jesus and our Father. I so often saw that love penetrate the lives of those who had been hurt and bruised by relationships that were less than loving and by a world that is insensitive to the real needs of men. Often, I would lift up my hands in praise and continually pray, "Lord, take all of me." My heart would feel warm and loving as I knew He had heard my prayer and would always walk with me in the work He planned. I knew that, as I continued to give more and more of myself to Him, the relationships He called me to love in and be loved in here and now would only become deeper, more loving and glorifying to

Him. Most of the time now I was walking in the heavens, continually praying both in my prayer language and with understanding, growing in power with the gifts of my Lord being more and more used and being filled more and more with a holy joy and peace. I felt the Spirit moving in and through me so deeply. I easily envisioned the gentle healing touch of Jesus. I walked the kingdom of God on earth—the sense of adventure we first learned through Ladd was now an everyday experience. I never questioned my emotional involvement in this which was strong and total, though often I wondered about my intellectual abilities since I've never considered myself to be an intellectual. Many times I have felt inferior to the task at hand. I never questioned my faith which was positive, undaunted, ever-present. It has never been tested by such questions as, "Does God really exist? Is God loving? Is Jesus really God's only-begotten Son? Was the Resurrection real? Is there a heaven and hell? Is life eternal? How do you know you're going to heaven? Are you sure God loves you? How do you know God loves you?" Nor in the last five or six years was my faith ever perturbed over the reality and work of the Holy Spirit, my personal, growing, loving relationship with my Father in heaven, and Jesus Christ alive and powerful in me. I knew I was a sinner, but to the dismay of some I seldom mentioned much about my sin. I was more comfortable sharing my sainthood and theirs in positive faith, for this was and is the reality of the kingdom and Spirit of God in our midst. All the years of my life were years of forward movement in my living with God and His Christ—ever increasingly loving, more powerful, more graceful, more believing, more Spirit-filled, more emotionally intensive, more giving, more secure. I had never rebelled against God in my whole life in the sense that I had never shared an angry word with Him, never despaired of His work; I had never doubted, always knew and usually felt emotionally and often dramatically His forgiveness of my sins. I often wondered why others had such struggles with these things and never understood how someone could actually become angry with the Giver of life. It always seemed to me that we had so much to be thankful for that we should only rejoice, praise God, put on love and joy, wear a continual smile and witness for Jesus. I tried to do just this and was so one with the source of this strength that I often assumed it was me, that it was my personality. I became short-tempered with those who relished conflict and tension and tried to avoid it myself with a passion equal to my growing love for the Lord. I recognized my sin but generally pushed it into the background, recalling it mostly as I heard the sins of others and was able, at least in pastoring, to always understand and never condemn. What I did not realize, as I became more and more actively hid in Christ, was that in a much different sense I was also becoming more and more hid in Adam. I was to learn of a helpful tool that served only to break my fall as I tumbled headlong off the summit of God's holy mountain.

Sin to Gift

The workshop was well-attended and the Spirit moved powerfully as the body came together to learn, to praise God and to lift up Jesus in their midst. It was the Atlantic City Conference of October, 1977, and we had gathered to hear the Linns, two brothers who had both entered the Jesuit priesthood, share their experiences of the Lord's work in their lives. Particularly important this day in their sharing was how He had taken their deepest sins and, through His transforming love, turned these sins into their greatest giftedness. They shared this as a profound principle of God's love and a way in which the people of God could understand the apostle Paul's statement of faith concerning the transformation of the whole man into the personality of God and the likeness of Christ.

I remember a comfort I felt unusually deep in my spirit that those large and awesome areas of sin in my life might yet budge. I knew that, by inviting Jesus to come into my heart and by giving light to every conceivable darkness within, someday the closet doors which I had so firmly bolted shut would have to open and He would see, as would I, the depth of my sin. I now felt, after this needed revelation to me of the way in which He deals with our sin as a follow-through of His original forgiveness, that indeed the promises of the Word are sure and without reproach, that the days ahead would see change in my life and that the inward sins of my heart would indeed be transformed.

As an aside, how often in our Christian experience things come toward us as new revelations—things which we had learned before in a different context, things we had heard and discarded at the time as not being relevant—ways in which the Lord, by His Spirit, prepares us for the deeper time of learning. I've often felt that I've learned some very important life lessons years after I should have known them or years after my peers had already discovered them. I have usually felt guilty that I did not see these things in the Word of God before or did not read it with enough attention and depth to learn the first time what I should have known. In a much more positive way, I'm continually amazed at how living and vibrant the Word is when we can literally read the same passages year in and year out and never cease learning new, life-changing realities, each time we read the familiar Word. We once heard Robert Frost, author of *Aglow With the Spirit,* speak on "the gift of imagination"—to be able to look beyond the literal words or experience and let your imagination go where the Spirit will lead it. As he proceeded in his talk, he illustrated how the Spirit let his imagination plumb new depths and understandings of very familiar words. He prefaced his remarks with, "Now let's imagine that this is what happened," and we wept as one new truth after another flowed out of his heart. He was gifted with imagination, directed by the Holy Spirit, bringing us all into deeper unity with our Creator. This in itself is an example of what I mean by "sin to gift." How often so many of us were told that an inquisitive mind, or an undisciplined mind, or a daydreaming mind, or even an idle mind could lead to trouble. And surely they can. But all these traits of the mind, under the guidance of the Spirit, can produce a giftedness that literally brings people into the temple courts of their God. How beautiful and exciting a Spirit-led imagination can be and how much more touching and warm to the human heart than our analytical theologies. Jesus spoke in parables for our time because He trusted in the imagination of men to sift out the truth of the kingdom.

I used to need to have things pretty well figured out ahead of their occurrence so there would be a minimum of surprises.

Furthermore, there was always a need for consistency in the understanding of how all things worked. This can lead toward a pretty dull existence if you're not careful. Well, true to form, I decided to list my greatest areas of sin to discover what the Lord would turn into my greatest areas of giftedness, and to see where He was going in my life and how He would use me. This was a time I should have used my imagination, but I didn't and I'm still learning from the surprises the Lord sent my way.

Williamsburg was the setting. Judy and I had a chance to have an uninterrupted week away, the first in many months, and quite unlike us, we first thought of the idea on a late Sunday afternoon in November and were on our way the next morning. We had always enjoyed Williamsburg, a frequent haven during our seminary years in Richmond, and it seemed natural to wend our way south and visit there again. Though we did not go for the express purpose that I should examine my sinful nature, it became more apparent to me as I shared with Judy about the Atlantic City conference and as we talked of the visit of Bob Whitaker on a teaching mission to our church that I take this opportunity to make a list of my sins and to contemplate the giftedness the Lord would bring to these areas. The Linn brothers had suggested we do this and here was the first real opportunity I had. They instructed us to list the worst, deepest sins we knew of, for these would become the areas of greatest giftedness.

My first list with two columns, the first for sins and the second for giftedness across from the sin, filled an eight and a half by eleven sheet and I still wasn't finished. If there ever was any humor or detached analyzing in this exercise, by the time I reached the bottom of the page it was gone. I ripped up the paper and threw it away now with a heavy heart. Even in faith I would end up with too much giftedness if I pursued this course of thought. As the Lord would have it, however, the maid's disposing of my torn-up paper in the trash the next day was not the absolution of my thoughts even though perhaps it was symbolic of the absolution of my sins. I was to write another list upon returning home. Even though this list was much shorter, it was to become a life-and-death struggle for me. I was not prepared for the oncoming battle because I had thought ever since my experience of being in hell after John's death, when the glory of Jesus' forgiving love filled the room, that I would never again experience that kind of death.

Spirituality and Humanity

As I was led to feel in new ways the consequences of the sins I had listed now for the second time, I experienced daily new convictions of the Holy Spirit and though they were gentle and non-condemning—still in the context of the Lord's work toward giftedness—it was all becoming a total and consuming experience for me. For the first time in my life, I began to sense the Lord becoming somewhat distant, going away from me, and sometimes seeming like He was in a distant mist of another time and place. Though I did not always feel close to Him nor always sense Him to be close to me in the past, there was always a feeling of forward movement. There were many times, for instance, after I knew His dramatic saving love through the experience of John's death, when I did my own thinking and planning, when I did not actively seek His Word or direction about particular things but never felt seriously convicted of this nor ever questioned His loving concern for me in spite of myself. After the baptism of the Spirit, however, I did indeed try to seek Him out in all things and He became a constant companion and co-worker in everything. I always sensed and knew His presence with every waking breath I took. My relationship with Him had always grown and become deeper—it was always forward gear, upward movement, greater spirituality.

What was happening now? He had never withdrawn like this before. Without sensing His presence, the conviction of my sin grew heavier day by day. New convictions were added, great and small. I tried, but more and more feebly, to keep faith with the thought that this was all a part of transforming me into a sharper instrument of His love and peace. Soon, however, even the vestiges of this faith were to go. Every day a new conviction would come, a new question would also appear that I knew was coming from Him and laid upon my heart: Can you give up this or that? Can you give up your dependence upon the vision? Can you give up your dependence upon the gifts? On and on it went until I believed I had given up every dependence I had. It was then I began to feel the loss of all the giftedness He had given. I was unable to love, to hope, to have faith. I stopped praying and listening to Him as I began to hear voices that sounded like His but couldn't have possibly come from Him. I could no longer pray for another's healing, for I had lost the faith for any particular act of His healing. I could not help others discern His will because I truly did not know what it was, except that He loved them. And finally I could not preach. I've never been able to preach about anything that was not confirmed in my own life—anything I did not know with 100 percent certainty. Now I knew I was certain about so little that one Sunday morning my sermon was literally one minute long. I believed I should never share doubts from the pulpit; indeed, I had never had that many and I felt I should not begin sharing such negative thoughts now. On the morning of my one-minute sermon I shared one verse from Scripture and said all that was within me believed it—as I truly did believe that if we asked He would answer, if we sought we would find and if we knocked He would open, if not at once then after we continually knocked. (I could not then say what He would answer or what we would find or what door would be opened to us but it would be something in the context of His love. That's all I knew for certain and that was such a struggle in faith that the night before, I was more heavily burdened over that sermon than with any one previously.) Under the pretext that all congregations need variety in preaching, I sat down. They loved that sermon and after ten years of preaching from that pulpit I think it's the one they remember the most. They will not know until they read this that it was the hardest one I ever preached.

I could not share what was happening to me. Where love had been, I found hate and resentment of longstanding that I never knew was there. Where hope had been, I found despairing, deeply depressive thoughts of the future; where faith had been I found unwillingness to fight; where power had been, I found emptiness and not caring; where vision had been, I felt deception and confusion; where certitude had been, I found doubt and bewilderment; where discernment had been, I found confusion and blindness; where the sense of the presence of Jesus Christ within me and the Holy Spirit's presence of released power had been, I found hell with its overwhelming darkness; where prayer had been, I found no purpose to go on.

I began to know a much deeper mystery to the sins I had placed upon my second list; the worst was pride, a driving need for respect and recognition, coupled with fears of rejection, emotional insecurities coupled with passivity and a need for strong attachments to people and in some cases past experiences. I began to discover that what I had done in all the years past was to spiritualize my humanity—not really letting it out for transformation but burying it under spiritualization. What I was seeing now was the depth of the mystery of sin and a full-blown picture of my darkest humanity. I saw the price others had paid for my sin—the casualities on the road of my growing spirituality. I was becoming bitter and selfish—wearing a mask outside when I had to, but inside I was seething with anger and confusion. Judy received most of my anger because she tried desperately to love me with a healing love but I, like a drug addict or alcoholic, had to reach rock bottom before I could receive love. I still could not share with others. Thanksgiving and Christmas went by and I could only see the ravages of hell. I internalized most of the blame and guilt—it was truly mine to bear—no one else had brought me to this point and I resented even more the situations that had caused me to get angry with Judy. Finally it was the Lord who received the broadside of my hostility, pain, and overwhelming anger. I had experienced hell; one day I felt particularly like Lazarus reaching out for a drop of water from the finger of Abraham and receiving none. That day I had trouble breathing, gasping for breath and feeling like I was choking most of the day. It was almost unbearable, accompanied by excruciating pain. I felt I had been condemned to this place for eternity. I saw the sin of Adam and its deep seed in me—I had tried to be God (never consciously but lurking within my human emotions and motives) and I realized how much I had desired to know all He knew.

There I was. I remembered the struggles between Saul and David and the Lord. I thought of Saul losing his mind, yet still serving the Lord. I remembered a sermon we studied in seminary,

"The Shipwreck of Saul." Though I felt no positive emotions at this time, and could not love or be loved, I felt negative emotions with great intensity and could relate in perfect oneness with "The Shipwreck of Saul," the trial of Job, the hanging of Judas.

And now at this point I think it's significant to mention some of the things the Lord allowed me to hang on to though no one alone nor all of them together formed a sufficient explanation for me to understand what He was doing.

In spite of traversing hell, doubting my own salvation, feeling utterly condemned and no longer a part of God's positive work, I did not once doubt His loving nature. (I found the worst kind of rebellion within me at this point because I was totally upset and angry at the way He was loving me. It was most comforting later, though, as healing began to take place and I read about a loving Father's chastisement of His sons and was profoundly grateful to begin to reestablish my sonship again.) Although I felt I knew Him no longer and that He had betrayed me, I never once doubted that Jesus was the Christ, the Son of God, the Savior of the world and, indeed, the Lord of all. Even though I was called to give up vision upon vision and gift upon gift and was rendered, I felt, useless, He allowed me to hang on to one vision, and one only—that Christians would only enter this new age as one—in one body of Christ. Although I felt my relationships were fractured badly with everyone, I knew Judy and I were to become even more united than we had been and that, if this alone were the goal I achieved, it would be according to His will. Even though I was pretty sure Satan was having a good time with me, I never could accept that the Lord, now so distant to me, did not still have His hand in all that was happening for some purpose that only He knew. And I knew shortly after I began my descent down the mountain that I was to resign my pastorate though I didn't know why nor was there at that moment a future ahead. Where was my real heart—the deep one, the one that lay fathoms under the one I had known all my life? This was the one I invited Jesus into and He came with His burning light. What did it really show? I remember sharing with Ron Scopel early in the fall that I was ready to go home—I had climbed the mountain and the Lord was very, very good. Excited about each day in this life, indeed, but if He was ready, so was I.

The Beginning of Healing

Angels came! The greatest was Judy who tried so hard to love me through this time and I could not deny the Lord was trying hard to love me through her. I wept very little during these days, for my heart was like stone and my mind was set. I had the worst case of rebellion all fall and winter. It was the first time I had rebelled in my life. My tears served to clean me out. Somehow I knew that would happen and I prayed a very short prayer asking for tears. About once every three weeks my eyes would fill up, especially when Judy would say something that let a very deep part of my heart know she understood. One night I allowed her to pray with me and for the first time in months the tears came and I felt the Lord trying to reestablish some contact with me. Another day Bonnie, our German shepherd, sat at my feet all day and the Lord spoke through her unknowing but faithful concern.

On another day the doorbell rang and Ladd was at the door. I hadn't seen him for two years. I hugged him long and hard. He could not have known the terrible anguish I was feeling. He could not have realized I felt like my world was crashing down all around me or that the Lord was step by step asking me to give up everything I cherished including all that He had given me. He could not have known that now the Lord had emptied me of all gifts save my knowledge that He was still with me, that He loved me and the peace that assurance brought. He could not have known that even that afternoon the Lord was preparing my heart to give up all ministry, a call I had known since I was a child. When Ladd was among us years ago many of us sensed a very special apostolic quality about him and somehow knew that when he spoke, it was the Lord speaking carefully-chosen words—just to us. We knew we had been in the presence of the Lord.

Ladd shared with me for over an hour and the Lord did indeed speak to me—but in a much different way than I had expected or ever experienced. It was, I remembered, Ladd who had shared with us years ago the adventure of being sons. We knew about being sinners so he naturally emphasized our sainthood and we dreamed dreams and saw visions and the glory of it all was likened to that of the Crusades.

Now Ladd again spoke from his own heart and experience of the word the Lord had confirmed in him. He was in the process of seeking secular employment. He needed to earn enough money to care for his wife, June, who was now recuperating from an operation. No doors of ministry opened to him. His days of mighty apostleship had drawn to an end and he was now called to care for a woman who had loved him so deeply over the years. He had already worked through the possibility of future resentment of the situation having robbed him of his ministry and place with the Lord and knew it now to be firmly the Lord's call to his heart. Then he said to me with tears of understanding and compassion in his eyes, "It's sufficient to know you're pleasing the Lord with your daily love for Him."

I fought being bitter with the Lord. This meeting with Ladd took place after I started my headlong descent but before I had been stripped of everything and cursed the day I was born. The Lord was already trying to send the balm of healing, cushioning my fall even before I would rail at Him in anger. While my passivity on the one hand was not allowing my anger to surface, my overwhelming pride was beginning to scream louder day by day. Could I give up the ministry? I loved it so much and found it so deeply satisfying. I had felt the incomparable joy of the Lord allowing me to be the vessel to bring others to Him (though few in number). I had prepared all my life for this.

The gentleness of this afternoon was to be followed by a painful wrenching within my soul when I realized in a moment of torment and anguish that my ministry had indeed caused casualties along the way and had become, in some cases, a block between the Lord and His love for those casualties. Though my mind had twisted all this at this point, I was never given the power to take His love from another person. Nevertheless, in that painful conviction, I was able to give up, indeed welcome, the loss of ministry to prevent any more hurt and, as I was feeling then, the possible judgment of having gifts to accomplish great things in the Lord save one—the love to never hurt those who loved me most.

I had grown to depend on my ministry as I had depended on people and things all my life. I knew the Lord wanted me to depend on Him first as I tried to do but because I didn't depend on Him enough, I was being asked to give up all the people and things I loved, even the giftedness and ministry He had given me.

I was reminded again in the Scriptures of Thomas and his need for proof, of Peter and his need to confess his love for Jesus three times and having to struggle each time with the thought that his love for other people, for the truths or even trappings of God, for the experiences of God or even his own life was greater than his love for Jesus.

The Lord sent another balm as the doorbell rang. Dan Nabor, general manager of Our Daily Bread Food Cooperative, came to visit with me. He told us of his days in the monastery and of a five-year period of his life there when he could not sense the Lord but only envisioned Him as a distant mist, mysterious and unapproachable. Dan rejoiced that he could also share with us two other things he had learned during this long desert period of his life; first, that the Lord has a beautiful and sensitive timing as He allows this experience in the lives of those He loves and has chosen, knowing precisely what each needs to see with new eyes; and that, secondly, when the Lord seems the farthest away, when He is shrouded from all our senses, when we ponder most deeply if He shall ever again walk with us, it is in this very time He is closest to us, ministering to our every need with a yearning love that seeks for us to learn, purely and only in faith, that He abides with us forever and shall never abandon us. Ever since I had met Dan I was aware that he generated a wonderful witness of always walking humbly with his God and was filled with an unsearchable joy. His life as well as the words he shared this day touched our hearts with new hope and purpose.

The Lord also spoke through the body of the church in many small, sensitive ways of loving kindness. As never before I was seeking His word and love through others and found that He gave it through them even though they had no idea of what I was experiencing.

Finally, there were a few people who so deeply laid down their lives for us and were so willing to help without even being asked. Through all my resentment and bitterness toward the Lord, I could not deny any longer the new fresh appreciation that was growing within me of His love through these special friends. Their commitments were sacrificial with no promise of my response and I knew the Lord was there.

There were some lessons to learn. I began to recover from the disease of rebellion as I stopped expecting some miraculous intervention which would answer all my questions and thereby set me free. Rather now was the Lord to deeply bless and honor the determined action of my will to reclaim or uncover the shrouded gift of faith He had given me so many years before and that now seemed totally inoperative. Together Judy and I made decisions we knew were right. Many things before us could be answered with common sense. Life was to become much simpler than before. Hundreds of areas in life are simply guided through Scripture. Many actions are scripturally right or wrong and only lend themselves to confusion if we want them to. Each step forward was a step of faith with no human guarantees but we began to discover the Lord was out on the water ahead of us. Somewhere we came across the thought that you can't steer a parked car so we decided to start the car moving without any of the previous guidance systems working and discovered that we had within us all along a much simpler trust in the Lord than we had supposed.

I had rediscovered the enemy. I learned that I could be deceived even in the things of God—Satan had done just that and the Lord had allowed him to. We would learn that the Lord intended us and other Christians to be more aware of the enemy than ever before and especially the potential deceptions within the very gifts of God themselves. Also we were to learn that the Lord never takes back what He has given in spite of the fact it may seem so, but He will deepen the guidance systems with greater discernment and truth if we are willing to allow Him. Not only is His love constant, even when our appropriation of it is not, but so too is His Word an ever-present, multifaceted gift we tend to overlook.

I learned that along with the Lord's love (I needed first to say as an exercise of my will and as a total statement of faith based solely upon the witness of the Word that He still loved me and, in great fear, that I loved Him. I say this to show how powerful the deception of Satan was because I had become so overwhelmingly convinced by everything I sensed around me at one point that the Lord did not love me and had indeed condemned me that I had become my own worst enemy) was simple truth, order, righteousness—all of which someday in our walk with the Lord are unavoidable. Even more exciting, however, was the experience of realizing that simple truth, order and righteousness are dear friends to the Christian.

And I learned how much I had presumed of and upon the Lord. I could now peacefully, joyfully and thankfully for the first real time in my life let the mystery of the Lord be mystery. He had revealed so much of himself to me through the Word and charismatic experience that I inadvertently assumed there were to be few mysteries left. When He became so distant to my senses, I could think nothing else other than the thought that the Lord was now the embodiment of mystery, not allowing me to presume anything and now meeting me only on top of the water, giving me the courage to take one tiny faltering step after another into His awaiting arms of love.

Finally, I learned that the movement of charism in these days is best described as a set of tools for us to lift up Jesus and proclaim Him with real, truthful, authoritative love that also forgives as His love did from the cross. The whole movement is to lead us effectively and powerfully to our Father and His kingdom and to receive the love He has for us that yearns and plans to make us one, that the whole world might know Jesus Christ was sent from Him. These things will outlast the movement, for they are of God. To be one with Him and His Christ in these days is to be one with each other as the body of Christ; a bride being prepared unblemished and unwrinkled, pure and spotless, expectantly awaiting her bridegroom.

Thank you, Father, for promising an everlasting love to your children and for caring enough about your sons and daughters to love them with a real love that does not compromise with any enemy. Thank you for healing our wounds when we have been hurt and for awaiting us always with open arms. Thank you for always being there as well as for the many gifts of your love that sustain us. In deep and heartfelt thanksgiving, Father, we love you and ask for the way to open before us as we express your love, through Jesus, for each other. Amen.

6

The Mirror of My Family

May you be strengthened with all power, according to his glorious might, for all endurance and patience with joy, giving thanks to the Father, who has qualified us to share in the inheritance of the saints in light. (Col. 1:11-12)

There are six of us in our family, five of whom walk on two legs and the sixth gets around on four. We could all be placed in the largest palace in the world (mom and dad, two daughters, one son and one dog), each given his own room to live in, a private bath and plenty of our own things to do, be told to settle in our rooms and then do anything we'd like to do. Within five minutes we would all be in the same room; indeed, we'd be sitting on the same chair expectantly waiting for someone to speak.

There are five saints in our family and one dog who is the object of each one's love and attention. Here is a glimpse of part of our family tree:

Dad and Mom Twitchell   Dad and Mom Herold
Warren (brother)   Nancy (sister)
Thomas born April 27, 1940   Judith born March 24, 1941

Joined in Marriage September 9, 1961
Kimberly Michelle born June 24, 1966, in Hagerstown, MD
Kenneth Sean born May 28, 1970, in Providence, RI
Rebecca Leigh born March 7, 1975, in Providence, RI

We could have made this diagram much larger but it shows that the Lord had to be doing a lot of thinking and planning just to work this all out.

Judy and I held hands all through the movie, *Inherit the Wind* with Spencer Tracy playing Clarence Darrow in the famous Scopes trial. This was on December 10, 1960, in downtown Syracuse. Though it was only eleven degrees outside and we had walked down and back from the campus we both felt warm as toast. The dialogue between Clarence Darrow and William Jennings Bryant was far different from that of *Beach Blanket Bingo*, maybe a more probable first date in our day, but when a point was made that we agreed with, we squeezed each other's hands (that's why we were holding hands). It was incredible—we agreed on everything. Judy and I had known each other since the beginning of the semester and had become pretty good friends but had never considered each other for a date. Even on this cold, wintery December night we were alone, apart from our other friends who were out on dates; we had decided earlier in the day that we would study together at the library. When we found it was closed that night, we were left with the dilemma of what to do. The movie finally took our fancy and, as the Lord would have it, we found the gift He had planned for each of us of a lifetime helpmate in each other that night.

Judy and I experienced a wonderful courtship. Since Christmas vacation was close to our first date and we would be going our separate ways for the holidays, we had no trouble justifying skipping all classes between the tenth and seventeenth when vacation would begin in order to spend the time sharing together over cups of coffee. I don't remember a time in my whole life when I would get up so early; I would go to Judy's dorm, throw pebbles at her screened window to wake her up and together we would spend the day until curfew, talking. This was a pure gift from the Lord and one for which we've always been thankful. Judy and I have always been able to share with each other, not as a discipline but rather as a joy, and we keenly feel the lack of it when we don't have time. We enjoyed each other's company from the very beginning, have always stimulated and challenged each other and have grown in and from our continual sharing.

By December 11, we knew we were to be married and though we still don't agree on that date (I think it was the eleventh; Judy thinks it was at least four or five days later), I remember the cold, wet snow soaking right through the knees of my trousers as I proposed to the most beautiful girl in the world—right out where the world could see—in front of the Art/Music/Architecture School on the front steps that my Dad had used each day to enter his classrooms thirty years before. Though I was a sociology major and had already learned at this point in my studies that such things just don't happen and that courtships should last years before a successful marriage could be predicted, I threw all surveys to the wind and, with great authority, beautiful love in my heart and certainty beyond all doubt, told Judy she was the one I wanted for life. I had more discernment in the Lord then than I knew anything about, for surely we were His gift to each other. This has been confirmed a million times over and I affirm it as excitedly now, almost eighteen years later. Our first task was to convince our parents of our discernment. (Of course, we didn't call it discernment; we didn't even know that word then; we called it what it was and is—love.) We told them we would save them money! It would be cheaper for us to live as married people together than as single people separately. We told them we would study more and I particularly might get off one dean's list (the wrong one) on to the other (the right one)—Judy was already on the right one.

Being both a pastor and a parent now, I can understand the fear and disbelief that immediately strike the heart at such claims but we were so determined that we must have hit them like a steamroller. The date was set, the chapel was secured and everything was put in order. Mark Twain once quipped that he couldn't frolic with mince pie after midnight. He conceded it might be all right for someone else, but it would probably kill him. I would probably never suggest that our brief courtship and early decision to marry be normative for anyone else. But for those young lovers who feel exactly like Judy and I did, let me add—we did save our parents considerable money that next year and for the first time in my college career, I did find my name on the right dean's list, and Judy and I were blissfully happy. As I look back now after the years, I can also truthfully affirm the many wonders of the Lord's timing as we grew together in love pretty much unhindered by the strains and stresses that pull at so many young marriages.

We have also learned together that growing into the unity and oneness the Lord has prepared for us will be a life-long process which doesn't conversely happen overnight nor does it happen without a love that's willing to sacrifice and be vulnerable. I'm convinced our Father intends marriage to be a joy, deeply and richly appropriated each day. It is meant to be the most fulfilling, helpful, supportive and dear human relationship we are to ever have. It is the one and best human relationship which teaches us the most about our relationship with Him, with His only begotten Son Jesus and with the Holy Spirit. It is the one relationship which cannot long harbor masks or self deceptions or false images. It is the one relationship which provides a constant, ever-present barometer of our feelings and understandings about ourselves, each other, other people, our God. It is the one human relationship which constantly sifts out any dishonesty or untruthfulness we perpetrate upon ourselves or, positively, which calls us to truth in every human experience. This can't be found if we choose only to live together without the binding covenant of marriage (an opinionated word for this generation) because the basic premise of such a relationship is wrong. Only in a binding marriage covenant can we thoroughly, deeply and responsibly work through the concepts of law that engender the deeper freedom that those who live together without contract believe they have achieved as a given. On another count, I'm equally convinced that the church still ought to be uplifting marriage and family as the basic covenant community (particularly within the charismatic movement) over and above all others. This is not just a matter of tradition; it deals with God's law and nothing that is happening today within the realm of the Spirit precludes the family as still being the first cell in the covenanted body of Christ. To go one step further, this likewise ought to be the place where single people may find their own needs more radically and realistically met for Christian community. I've found no other place where I can so tenderly learn the ever-deepening truths of the gospel as it applies to my life—the truths of love from the cross, of my Father's unconditional, irrevocable covenant of love for me, the truths of Christian freedom that allow me each day to recommit my life not out of law but out of thanksgiving in a free-will response to covenant, the truths of accountability, discipleship, authority, sensitivity, discernment and wisdom, the truths of commandment love (John 15:12-17) and gospel love (John 3:16).

Judy and I have wept and laughed together; we have hurt each other and blessed each other; we have been real to each other even to the point of admitting that there have been times we could not live with ourselves—how indeed could the other live with us? We have often heard the Lord in each other, I particularly so and quite honestly have fought tooth and nail against what I've heard until somehow, in some way still mysterious to me, the Lord enables me to hear, accept change, and offer thansgiving. And I'm amazed that Judy has shared with me these things all along. Often I have accepted the same word she has shared (sometimes literally over the years) from a book I've read or another person I wouldn't dare refute. I'm then immediately thankful, mad, and ashamed of my stubborn pride. But because Judy loves me as she does, I'm left with my dignity intact. Over the years this has been a very healing experience for me, for I discovered many years into our marriage how very hard I thought I needed to fight for Judy's respect. I would invariably do the things which would normally cause a blow if not a death for the respect she had for me, and would discover she still respected me nevertheless. This showed me that my worst enemy was my own lack of respect for myself. All along that's what I was really testing and battling and the Lord spoke through the tender, dependent love of my wife that had to be there over all the years for His voice to be heard in spite of myself, saying, "Tom, I love you no matter what you do." If more wives could tell their husbands this and if more husbands could tell their wives this (and obviously mean it) the Lord would zoom into the marriage faster than the speed of light.

Judy and I take ourselves pretty seriously but we've also had some fun with very serious things (as we look back). I would like to mention one because again I believe it's not just for us. Some years ago we devoted ourselves totally to the scriptural advice of Paul that wives should submit to their husbands and husbands should love their wives in a manner analogous to the church's submission to Christ and Christ's love for the church. We tried very hard. The seriousness of the subject can be seen even by the casual observer in many writings within the charismatic community as opposed to the movement of ERA across the nation. And it was indeed so real to us that we often engaged other couples in debates that probably scared them. It was also very important in the sense that I particularly needed to grow in sensitive, loving authority as opposed to my passive nature which often looked like I didn't care. Judy worked at it so hard that she was in greater submission to me than I've seen any church be in submission to Christ. I felt like I'd been elevated to the rank of general in the army and Judy was a private under my command. As we progressed along this road, Judy became nearly directionless on her own and I became more like a general every day, mostly resenting my increasing power. Suffice it to say, our little army so constructed didn't win many battles. We were, I believe, where the Lord wanted us then because we held our defenses, one general and one private, but we weren't an invasion force by any stretch of the imagination. Since then a new manual has taken shape. The Lord Jesus is the source of authority and His love is the weapon of His authority. Judy's love for me is no less His love from the cross than mine for her and there are just as many times I need to listen to her as she does to me because it's coming from Him. We have discovered the joy of submitting to the Lord in each other. And, truthfully, I must admit that as general of the army, the troops and I marched right off the cliff too many times for me to sit in headquarters alone.

The law of God and the Spirit are consistent with each other. From Genesis to Revelation the story places a man and woman together to be one. But that oneness includes diversity, needs, strengths, gifts, and failings that are peculiar to the couple. The Spirit of God sees a human being to love and be empowered before

He sees male or female. Only as we see and listen to the Lord in each other, do husband and wife together discover new depths of submission to the Lord and understanding of His love from the cross. Husbands and wives are responsible to each other and their family for spiritual growth. Together both are to discover their weaknesses and failings and submit them to the Lord for transformation. We are only free as we become slaves to Christ, something of freedom even the ERA can't understand but likewise husbands can learn much about freedom as they submit to the Lord in their wives and then take headship and authority in the family. The centurion spoke to Jesus of his understanding of both giving and receiving orders. Because of this he had the faith to receive the kingdom through healing. Though I still exercise headship in the family most of the time and Judy feels secure in this, we're in the field side by side.

As we were both jewels to our parents, precious and without price, so too are our children to us. Again, and especially, are they the mirror of our beautiful relationship with the Father in heaven. Through our three children, we have learned some wonderful things about the way our Father loves us. These things are open to all parents if they are willing to look. First of all, there are three children for us, all of whom were planned for and expected in joy. They are all different but immediately we loved them, even before they were born. We love them all with the same abiding love but knew immediately after Ken, our second child, was born that the love we had for each was to be a specialized love because each child's personality is so unique. We are keenly aware of the times when our love has been deficient as well as the times when it has been good and I continue to marvel as I relate this knowledge to my understanding of our Father in heaven who never fails in His love for all His children, who never is deficient and who never lacks the time or wisdom to love us as we need. As good as our love might be at times, I'm gratefully aware that His for all of us is better. When our children are disobedient or rebellious we discipline them but we never stop loving them. Our hearts forgive them very easily even though the discipline may be severe and there is always a new day, always a second chance, always a fresh start. When I think how imperfect this is in me yet how perfect in Him, I melt away and once again come back to my Father both as the prodigal and also as the son who stayed home, knowing in my heart He has not forsaken me any more than I could forsake my own children.

Kim, Ken and Becky are all beautiful children and each is a very special gift to us. Their personalities are all very different and unquestionably they bear the marks of their mom and dad while still being individuals. Even at two and three weeks of age certain little personality traits began to take shape. They know their Lord Jesus and have a flowing natural relationship with Him. They are developing a sense of God's fatherhood and we try to point them there whenever we can.

Also emerging within Kim and Ken is a loyalty and pride in their family. Becky says, at three, she is proud too, but with such a winsome look in her eye that we know we're in for something when she says it.

There are conflicts and Kim wanted me to be sure to mention that problems exist as well as loving solutions. One particular thing we've found helpful as we all relate together is the simple truth that Jesus lives in us and when we hurt each other, we hurt Him too. Often Kim and Ken have forgiven each other through tears of genuine remorse.

When Becky arrived at birth with deformities in her hand, a special love developed immediately from Kim and Ken and the day we brought her home from the hospital, I've never witnessed such a tender and awesome love as I saw in them for her. They have been her responsible teachers ever since and we've never even needed to encourage their care and play with her. They have given naturally and beautifully since that first day.

Judy and I have devoted ourselves to answering their questions as honestly as we know how and sometimes it's painful for us to do so because we're open then to admit our own mistakes. There is surely a beautiful fruit, however, in that we love each other as very real people.

Though there is no question in the kids' minds as to who holds authority in the family, Judy and I try to be particularly sensitive to the Spirit in them, too, and we've noticed that there is an

The Mirror of My Family

uncanny sense of truth and discernment as they speak to one another or us. Though they are children, there are times when we all appreciate their wisdom and always I've thanked God for their simple trust in Him as their Father and Jesus, their very real and ever-present Brother.

I can imagine Jesus saying, "The kingdom of heaven is like the family. It is in this set of relationships you will discover a father's love, a mother's sacrifice, a child's trust. Together shall there flow healing and truth. Within shall be soft tears of forgiveness as the dignity of each is guarded. Joy shall be known in the growing moments of unity. Love shall set free as covenant bonds are strengthened and each one submits to God's love in each other. In this picture of the kingdom, love does not fail and the precious fruit of life is borne."

Like most parents, Judy and I are concerned about the future welfare of our children. But our concern often runs counter to what we experience around us. We tend to discipline more than many others and take a very active interest in the stimuli that reach our children all the way from various occurrences in the neighborhood to the shows they watch on TV. We believe that most of what the world tells parents and children is subtly and deeply deceptive, taking away from the realities of life and the Spirit. We lament the situations so prevalent today that call upon a much earlier maturity and discernment in our children than has ever been required. There are numerous persons in our community as well as most communities throughout this country who are bent upon destroying our children whether through drug addiction or cultic activities, or other means. Some of these persons are just individually sick but others belong to an organized force of deception. Let me only suggest here that Judy and I believe we cannot ever be too discerning or aware of the forces against family life, marriage and children. The support, affirmation, teaching, love and truth that parents are called upon to give their children today just to prepare them for the next few months ahead at any given time are greater than ever before, for our children are being called upon to be very wise indeed.

Life today is a radical commitment. If we don't choose it and pursue it actively we will be victims of death. By sitting still and letting things happen we will be chewed up and never know what hit us. Because something has become a time-worn institution such as the church or family, that by no means guards its safety today. It is one thing to be critical in the context of life and ever seek improvement in the flow of loving both church and family—it is quite another to give up and sit back or try other ways. Church for church's sake? Family for family's sake? Yes! If we're talking about life. Church is the body of Christ (at least in part—even in these days). Family is God's law and plan for the happiness of mankind. Praise God!

Thank you, Lord, for my family. How intricate and loving your plan for us is. Thank you for placing us all together to love and be loved. Thank you for the continual lessons of love you teach us as we wake up to each other and you each day.

Father, protect your little ones and let none harm them. Teach us as parents to be ever vigilant in love. Surround each marriage and family with the protective bubble of your love as you teach them in these days to be aware. Father, may all our relationships whether in family or elsewhere be a glory to you and your Son Jesus Christ. Amen.

PART II:

Unity Within the Body of Christ

7

United Presbyterian Church—
A Congregation of Mission

And now I am no more in the world, but they are in the world,
and I am coming to thee. Holy Father, keep them in thy name,
which thou hast given me, that they may be one, even as we are
one. (John 17:11)

Difficult Times

We followed the Allied moving van through the dark of the
night in one of those reflective moods that knows the bridges of the
past will only be traversed in memory and the streams and rivers
ahead will only be forded with new methods, new materials, new
life. Hagerstown had given us three good years. It provided a
peaceful and serene transition from seminary. Seminary studies
were so different from the work of the church and the years in
Hagerstown helped to prepare us for further ministry. In the calm
of that transition, Kim came into our lives as our first-born
daughter, so very much expected and desired and so very much a
joy and a fulfillment. We remembered the going-away party the
church had prepared for us and the many good wishes in spite of the
fact that I had thought, especially in my last year, that my sermons
had bitten hard into the sensibilities of the people and that we had
moved into a more radical phase of ministry in social action. As we
sped through New York City in a record twenty-five minutes, we
knew we had left the southern way of life for the first time in six and
one-half years and were headed for a fast-paced Yankee city where
problems were hard-core and raw, where personalities were not so

genteel, and where challenges would meet us every step of the way as I assumed the pastorate on my own for the first time.

We arrived on a cold, gray winter's day—December 13, 1968. The city was bleak and the air was damp inside the seventy-five-year-old, cape-styled manse—but our spirits were undaunted. The formalities of the call had already transpired over three separate visits we had made to Providence since the fall, so I would begin immediately with the work at hand of getting to know the people, preaching, and discovering the new paths in which we would walk. In our previous visits we had already discussed with the pulpit committee the basic problem the church faced. We had also discussed our basic style of ministry, with the crucial ingredient that we both felt distinctly called of God to enter into this union of work together. By the time of installation, January 5, 1969, we had already passed our first New England Christmas and found the people of the church were most gracious and friendly as they helped us through this time of year when families and old friends gather. They were our new family and friends and all during the holiday they brought us food, gifts for Kim and us, and their hands reached out to us in warmth and friendship.

Rev. J. Russell Butcher, my senior pastor and mentor in the Hagerstown church for three and one-half years, preached the sermon at the installation and service of worship formally inaugurating the relationship of congregation and pastor, a time of serious and solemn pledge that is to last the duration until God sees fit to call the pastor to a new charge and the congregation to a new challenge, whenever that may be. The church was full and the occasion a happy one for us all. I was thankful for many things, not the least of which was Rev. Butcher making the long trek northward to show our new congregation that the past years had been good ones as would be the hope and promise of the next. It was also a time, had there never been one before, when the umbilical cords of life's support were finally and completely severed and we were on our own with our God. So it was that in one of the coldest, wind-filled, ice-covered winters in my memory we began at the ages of twenty-eight, twenty-seven and two (and also with a newly acquired puppy who moved into the manse two days after we did) a life in the Lord that has moved from one age burning out as embers to the birth of a new age beginning with new fire in a church that now only slightly resembles what it was when we came.

The church in Providence started in 1893, meeting in the living rooms of Presbyterians who were raised in their strict and holy faith in Scotland. In two short years these devoted sons and daughters of John Knox's faith had built a church sanctuary and manse that would meet the future head-on with grace and strength. Indeed, it was to the original buildings, with a 1931 addition of a large gymnasium and meeting rooms, that Judy and I came in 1968. This church plant was still meeting the needs of the congregation and neighborhood three-quarters of a century after it was built. The 1931 addition was the result of a merger with another Presbyterian church approximately a mile away. This merger provided funds for a truly visionary ministry that might have seemed somewhat frivolous in that day.

The first sermons I preached in the church were primarily to people who were a part of that 1931 merger, or some who had joined the church as children prior to the merger, or to a few of their remaining sons and daughters. From 1893 until the mid-1950s the church experienced a steady growth pattern and at one time reached approximately 600 members. From the late fifties until our arrival, it had experienced a steady decline in membership until the 223 number on the rolls at my installation time. Much of the membership was of Scotch or Scotch-Irish descent; some were Dutch, English and Swedish. A goodly portion of the people had come to Providence and to this particular neighborhood via Nova Scotia as a result of the helping hand of relatives who had settled in Providence ahead of them. It was natural for them to move in on a weekday and be found in church on the following Sunday, becoming active members on the first possible occasion.

Following the war years, the church was to experience what so many inner-city churches did in that time. Young families moved to the suburbs and built their own churches, came back home for the holidays, but lived out their lives five to fifteen miles away from their home church. Some of the young families hung on for the sake of their parents and they were still there when we came.

Everyone recognized the next years ahead would be difficult years and filled with challenges that would call upon the greatest devotion and dedication of the congregation and its new young pastoral family. The stability of the church was somewhat dependent upon the stability of the neighborhood. In this case the church had historically depended upon long-term commitments from a nucleus of families and their extended families, and it was to undergo a severe test. Financially, the budget had never been great (perhaps because of traditional Scotch austerity) but it would need to become even more austere. The minister I was following had been pastor of the church for the previous sixteen years and had just retired from this church. He left a congregation that was solidly grounded in faith. They cheerfully gave small amounts which were tithes of small incomes. These people were, to be sure, the salt of the earth, honest and up-front. They had fellowshiped together for many decades but they were a people who, along with us, were not expecting all the changes ahead nor young enough in some cases to be resilient.

Planned Solutions and Unplanned Answers

In 1976 the United Presbyterian Church, USA (UPCUSA) completed a two-year study entitled "Church Trends." This report was given to the General Assembly meeting of that year in Baltimore. In the report, the special task force that was set up to undertake the study shared with the commissioners all of their data substantiating findings concerning church growth and decline patterns, which had been collected from a large random sampling of church congregations in the UPCUSA denomination. The report exploded many myths, pricked a lot of balloons and left many commissioners to that assembly dazed or unbelieving. The major results were (1) church growth or decline did not depend substantially upon its location, particular theological view, the church's involvement or lack of involvement in social action/community groups, the church's involvement or lack of involvement in the charismatic renewal and Holy Spirit baptism, the pastor and/or programs of the church, etc.; (2) that an overwhelming majority of people first came to the church they eventually joined at the invitation of a neighbor or friend or work associate who was a member of that congregation; (3) that growth or decline in membership of a congregation related directly and overwhelmingly to one factor—and one factor alone—the degree of warmth and friendliness of the people in the congregation.

Our planned solutions to meet the conditions that faced the church were numerous. The congregation had already taken one significant step in calling a pastor who was young and active, who believed as they did in the seriousness of Jesus as the Christ, but who also believed in integrating people of all backgrounds into the whole. Together we decided to make an all-out thrust toward the youth who were still remaining in the congregation and their friends in the community, toward the community itself to discover ways in which we might be helpful and also ways in which we might draw in further support, toward the languishing families in the congregation in an attempt to revitalize their interest, toward continued pastoral concern for the elderly and shut-ins, and toward united efforts with other churches (particularly Presbyterian) where such programs might be mutually beneficial. Toward these ends we began an active youth fellowship with the six young people in our congregation. We began a young adults'/couples' club with the remaining four couples in the church and three or four singles of that age bracket. We instituted programs of visitation several times to reach out to inactive families who were still on the rolls. We sought out fellowship with other churches. We reached out into the community—the beginnings of local mission efforts. We made periodic visits to the elderly and shut-ins. These are not unusual programs; no one would question their initial wisdom; they, each one, played out their life and left us with a still declining membership.

The youth fellowship took ahold and flourished for five years. We did a number of very worthwhile things together and there are still fruits in the lives of those who were deeply involved. The group grew to about thirty. Three of the original six remained active. The rest were Roman Catholics and since we were committed not to proselytize, we bent over backwards to preserve the heritage of all in the group. There were no new Presbyterians in the making.

The young adults' fellowship met for nearly a year and made a valiant attempt at all that was good. There was no lack of creativity or challenge. Due to the lack of homogeneity, however, commitment waned and the group died a natural death before it ever walked. Members in the group only saw one another on Sundays, lived miles apart from each other, and held only one thing in common—their church membership.

The inactive families we visited in hopes that a new pastoral face, a new sense of involvement, a new thrust in the church, might revitalize their Christian commitment showed little response. We kept trying in the interest of some of the elders but were to find repeatedly that these people had all left the church for specific reasons and those reasons were still there, even though a new pastor had come. They had no intention of coming back. I was surprised at the number on the roll who fell into this category and who were probably lost to Presbyterianism at least in our little church long before they ever joined the first time. We finally dealt with the majority of these people years later by offering one more chance (and this time I must say a serious confrontation was presented, not in terms of the church but in terms of their commitment to the Lord). Then we removed their names from the rolls of the church.

We extended hands to the other Presbyterian congregations in the city of Providence but basically found ourselves by this time all busy in our own neighborhoods, with our own fellowships, etc. We discovered a curious thing—many members would pass other Presbyterian churches to reach the one they attended. There are only three Presbyterian churches in Providence, with a fourth one near the city line. In 1968 all four pulpits were vacant. They were all filled within the year and were basically about their own business in spite of the presbytery's attempt to draw them together. Interestingly enough, by 1979 they all were vacant again. We also extended hands to two American Baptist churches whose hands were also outstretched.

We went into the neighborhood with fairly pure motives of helping the poor in their struggle for a better life and this perhaps of all our plans flourished the most, is still active and a large ingredient in what makes up the United Presbyterian Church in Smith Hill.

We visited the shut-ins and elderly and were refreshed ourselves as we returned home. Many of them held rich deposits of the faith. They had endured suffering and trials and had lived to tell of the Lord's victory through smiling eyes.

It wasn't long before my time was consumed by all that's mentioned above and the endless variety of things to which these activities led. So entrenched had I become that by the time some of the unplanned answers came, it was difficult to be responsive and shift gears. In my youthfulness I often lacked wisdom and foresight and would not concentrate on the right priorities. On the other hand, I was full of energy, saw my work as one total integrated whole and was highly motivated. I did best the things I enjoyed and was well-matched with the church's need for youthful leadership, radical community commitment, radical youth commitment, ecumenical concerns. Less well matched was I for the pastoral care and authoritative and administrative leadership the church also needed. This was, of course, to cause problems in the midst of which the Lord had His own ideas. He was to bring about changes that took all my waking hours to cope with; little wonder some of the people in the church found the changes imponderable. If success were to be measured in numbers and budgets, I would have walked the plank long ago. The 223 who started with me dropped to 140. Of the 140, about sixty were new faces. The budget of $21,000 when I came, dropped to an even more austere figure of $18,000. Only once in the years of my pastorate did we go over the top and then by a mere $101. The building now looks worse than it did then. But the Lord was to prepare and bring together a people who were poor, deeply experienced and well educated, sensitive and alert, and with an unequaled dedication to Him and His poor. He was to empower us along the way with the releasing of His Holy Spirit within us and give us the baptism we so deeply needed. He was to bring about healings we did not expect, send angels unawares, strengthen all our existing relationships with all other churches and friends, provide literally hundreds of friends and well-wishers of the church, send teachers and apostles from all over the country, increase our faith daily, work within us a love which was winsome—all this and much more. All of this together, however, was not to increase our membership figures or ever provide more wealth than we needed. We were never able to dream of increased resources in terms of great numbers of people nor did our minds ever work on any plans of spending seed money here or there to begin new ministries. We were to learn rather to endure with what we had by the inspiration of the Holy Spirit, to be faithful and patient within the limitations that were set upon us, and to grow in the spiritual stature of our Lord Jesus. I confess there were times this was discouraging as we would read of other phenomenal growth patterns in other churches. There were times when we would submit to a despairing or negative spirit and the undercurrent of this was always devastating. Balance was usually hard to achieve between those who would recognize what was wrong and those who never saw such things. Ground for unity within the body of Christ in our church was always hard-fought ground, slowly secured inch by inch. Signs of outward renewal were usually covered and subdued, with emphasis upon both the inward renewal of the Spirit, and tremendous sensitivity toward those who were offended or not ready for the outward display of gifts. Thus the baptism of the Spirit visited upon our congregation was to take on very subtle hues within which could be found both wisdom and sensitivity as well as fear and half-truths.

"But we have this treasure in earthen vessels," wrote Paul, "to show that the transcendent power belongs to God and not to us" (2 Cor. 4:7). "He is the image of the invisible God, the first-born of all creation; for in him all things were created, in heaven and on earth, visible and invisible, whether thrones or dominions or principalities or authorities—all things were created through him and for him. He is before all things, and in him all things hold together. He is the head of the body, the church; he is the

beginning, the first-born from the dead, that in everything he might be pre-eminent" (Col. 1:15-18).

So often we read of only the visible successes. Seldom do we read of those, for instance, who genuinely praise the Lord in and for all things yet who continue to suffer particular hardships. Likewise, seldom do we read of churches that still have struggles and challenges while walking in the Spirit. But we must look at these things too, for our Lord is still speaking; He is speaking in full truths, not half-truths; His love yet pours out for those churches and people yet unhealed, and it is not for the church to witness only to success, never looking at the failures, but to speak the truth, fully and in positive faith, boldly and in love, for our God truly is a God of love. He loves most of the time through earthen vessels of a human nature, again to show forth the fact that He is preeminent in everything. We must not be afraid of this.

Over thirty-five years ago in the rolling hills surrounding Northridge, Massachusetts, Clara Casperson, a member of the church for over twenty years at that time, attended a retreat seminar in the Dwight L. Moody campgrounds. She heard David du Plessis speak about Pentecost; he was, furthermore, to pray over her and she was to receive a precious gift. She returned to the church on Smith Hill and told no one of her experience for nearly thirty years but simply and quietly interceded all those years for the Lord to come and baptize His people with the power of the Holy Spirit. Every time David would come to Providence to Zion Bible Institute, Clara would go alone from our church to hear him and they became good friends. Undoubtedly in all those many occasions of sharing she had asked David to pray also for the outpouring of the Spirit upon our church. The Lord promised He would and through the faithful intercession of His chosen servant Clara, He sent His promised Spirit upon the people He had gathered together. Yes, thirty-five years later.

Healings and Learnings

Though it was unknown to us prior to the outpouring of the Spirit, the Lord had already begun the process of drawing together a body of people who would be responsive to His Spirit. Clara shared with Judy and me that she sensed in the very beginning that we were the ones the Lord had sent. She was on the pulpit committee and after meeting us, she interceded even more fervently. Judy would be the first one in the church to receive the baptism. She added her quiet intercession to Clara's—for me and for the church.

Greta O'Rourke would be next. Judy and Greta had become friends and Greta shared our concerned work as a congregation through the Capitol Hill Interaction Council. She began to attend a Bible study we held jointly with the United Baptist Church. One evening Greta asked Judy and me to pray with her in our living room and, although I knew nothing of what I was praying for and Judy did, the Lord gave Greta a beautiful baptism gift. Shortly after this, Greta joined the church through reaffirmation of her faith that was first found in the Episcopal church. Greta's ethnic background is Swedish.

Greta and Judy then began intercessory prayer together very early every Friday morning in the church sanctuary. I would be the next one to enter the new realm of the Spirit.

Following me was Dorothy Lusignan. We prayed with her in our living room. Dorothy had been drawn to the church earlier and had joined through her teen-age youngsters' attendance in the youth fellowship, the only person from that entire youth fellowship experience who was to make this kind of church membership commitment. Dorothy had been a young girl in Germany during the war. She was of Lutheran background and became a citizen of this country in the fifties, coming here with her American husband who had been stationed in Germany with the occupational forces. Dorothy was also one with us in the church's work in the Capitol Hill Interaction Council and became deeply involved as did Greta. Dorothy, like Greta, had been a resident of Smith Hill for many years. She had also attended the Bible study conducted jointly with the Baptists.

Next would be Bill and Cynthia Hernandez who started coming to the church through Cynthia's mother whom I had met and worked with in connection with OEO programs in Providence. Though Cynthia's mother lived in a different neighborhood and was involved in other kinds of work, she was aware of the Capitol Hill Interaction Council and of our church. She encouraged Bill and Cynthia to come. Bill was already steeped in pentecostalism. Cynthia's background was Baptist—but with soul. Bill was a Portuguese black and Cynthia was an American black. They also lived in Smith Hill and Cynthia was to receive more as she was prayed with in the Spirit.

By now the emphasis of our prayer meetings had changed. Years before we had begun, a Bible study combined with prayer with the United Baptist Church. Our prayer life in the midst of this was changing radically, enough so that we decided it was right to institute our own prayer meeting. Barbara Muniz was the only member of the church at this time who claimed the baptism of the Spirit who had grown up there as a young girl and who transferred with us into the new prayer meeting that was opening to the gifts of the Spirit. The prayer meeting would now begin drawing others.

Dick and Rita Gehrenbeck were to come into a relationship with the Spirit which moved us all. Dick and Rita had come a few years before from the Midwest. They had joined our church immediately upon their arrival in Providence and were just as immediately involved in the church's life and its particular missions through the Capitol Hill Interaction Council. When they moved to Providence, they selected a home midway between Dick's work and our church so they could be active in both without transportation problems. They are the only family who joined our church during my entire pastorate there who were born and raised as Presbyterians and who had basically the same upbringing as Judy and I did in the church. Dick is of German background; Rita is Swedish. They had attended prayer meetings off and on but were still somewhat skeptical of the experience. Dick became ill and within a matter of a few short days he entered the hospital for a rushed kidney operation to remove a large tumor. Dr. George Coleman, their next-door neighbor and leading New England cancer surgeon, observed the operation. The night before Dick's operation, we came together in prayer and, as a body, were perhaps more united than we had been at any other time in my memory.

We had just learned that we could ask our Father for what we wanted deep in our hearts. This was particularly significant for Rita who always felt these prayers might be selfish and shouldn't really be prayed. But we did all pray the deep desire of our hearts and in an unusual outpouring of love agreed in prayer that Dick would come out of the operation all right. Some were assured that night that he would be healed, some that he would indeed be all right. Rita sensed in her spirit that there would be good news the next day. Dick lay in his hospital bed reading *Power in Praise* by Merlin Carothers for the first time and underlining thought after thought that touched deeply his heart. He and Rita had already talked that afternoon about the eventuality of his death, remembering the good life the Lord had given them. They had three fine children, had served their first three married years on the mission field of Lebanon, had met in high school and fallen in love there in a childhood romance. Their families had always been the very best of friends and members of the same Presbyterian church in White Bear Lake, Minnesota. They were beloved by all in our church and, even in precharismatic days, they had given a boost to the morale of everyone. They were certain that our church would be blessed in its struggle to be the emissary of Christ in these difficult days.

The next morning in the hospital corridor one of Dick's colleagues who had been the first to hear the results of the operation saw Rita and ran to her with open arms. "I have good news," he told her. As they both wept, he shared that the doctors had operated and nearly cut the kidney in half trying to locate the tumor they had seen on the x-rays but they could no longer find. This experience opened the hearts of many and by the time spring flowers were in bloom we traveled into New Hampshire for a weekend retreat with some of the longtime members of the church as well as the now growing number of new faces and friends.

Ken and Catherine Gilroy went on this retreat. They had been members of the church since 1928. Their active involvement in the church had spread over the years into a paragon example to all of us of the Lord's faithfulness and perseverance in His love for His people. Ken had served many terms as an elder and Catherine had assumed leadership of the choir and church organist's ministry in the 1950s. On this weekend the Lord was to bless them with a well-deserved gift of joy.

Over a period of two and one-half years we all attended five retreats in which the Lord moved powerfully through healing and teaching. This was the instrument through which He drew others and since these retreats were always open, He often brought neighborhood people or members of other churches and we all shared in each other's joy. In the retreat prior to Dick's healing, Mary Jones and her family came. Her son Anthony fell into the icy waters of a nearby New Hampshire mountain lake on the Sunday afternoon of the retreat weekend. Clothed in a heavy woolen coat, he was unable to swim. His heavy boots dragged him down. The third time he surfaced for air, Donald Lusignan, Dorothy's son, pulled him out of the water and back into the canoe with super-human strength. At the same time, without knowing about these events, back at the main lodge we were in small groups, some discussing, some praying. Judy had opened the Scripture to Paul's shipwreck and didn't know why she was led to pray. Mary Jones sensed something was happening and was also led to pray. After it was all over we all knew that Anthony would have drowned except for the direct intervening hand of the Lord. Mary had joined the church prior to this because she was drawn not only to our work in the neighborhood but because she felt an acceptance and warmth. Mary, who is black, was another one of those Baptists with soul from the churches of North Carolina, and was now blessed with still a different kind of baptism.

There wasn't one retreat that failed to witness a miracle of the Lord. There was never a prayer meeting where He wasn't present. Our prayer meetings grew and for a while became an instrument of the Lord's healing for those who came. Separations began to subside as we learned to pray together—for each other audibly.

Another evening while we were still praying in our living room, Bob Nigohosian dropped by on college vacation and we prayed with him. Bob had been a member of the church since he was a small child. Upon graduation he was to come back to us, take up residence in Smith Hill, marry one of the young women from St.

Patrick's and become the first executive director of the Capitol Hill Interaction Council. Bob is Armenian and is an elder in the church. The prayer meetings moved to the church and still grew. Others came. Linda Darling, who is Syrian and was a member of the Ann Arbor community, along with Matt Steward, from a Scotch and American Baptist background, were to assume music leadership in the meetings. They lived in the neighborhood and both became elders.

Jeanine Jorian, a French Catholic who had also lived through the war years as a child in France and immigrated to this country after the war, was drawn to fellowship with us too. She received the baptism, and joined the church.

Cathy Warford White, an Irish-English Catholic by background who had not attended church for many years, came one Sunday morning. Already baptized, she joined the church soon thereafter. Some time after joining, Cathy's situation became such that we (Judy, Cathy and I) decided to try a modified household living arrangement and embarked on several months of not only learning about one another pretty deeply, but also discovering how the Lord can profoundly bless people who are sharing their lives together. We all grew in insights about ourselves as we learned to share more openly with each other. We all learned new levels of tolerance and intolerance that we would not have otherwise known, and we all learned a deeper love that was not only willing to sacrifice in certain areas but which became grounded and centered in truth. Though Cathy is now many miles away from us there is a unique bond with one who is part of us.

Jim and Jane Huddart, English folks from the Anglican Church, were prayed with and baptized. They then joined our fellowship. Pat and Ernie Droth, of German background, had no church ties. They were baptized and they became members too.

J.B. Maw, an Indian Mormon and his wife, Carol, who had been a Baptist were neighbors across the street from the church. They had been seeking the Lord since childhood. After they joined our church, most of Carol's family also joined. This came about largely through her continual intercession for them. David and Cheryl Rinaldi, who came from Catholic and Assemblies of God backgrounds, were married in the church. They felt their church home was as important as their relationship with each other.

And on the list goes. People from every conceivable background, race, national origin, religious training, profession, history of life experiences. Hardly any joined the church because it was a Presbyterian church but all loved Jesus and knew His love for them. All believed in miracles and saw them happen in their own lives. All brought to the body a gift to share. All came thirsting for fellowship with the Lord's people and found it in each other. All were willing and did indeed lay down their lives to lift up another. Most became involved in our work in and through the Capitol Hill Interaction Council. All were poor, yet they felt they were still more fortunate than others. (By "poverty" I mean that many only earned six to eight thousand dollars a year, even with large families.) All maintained active involvement in the church's life.

Our unity very definitely was grounded in Christ. These people were all Christians first. Whatever else they were was secondary. This was the impetus for many healing relationships. Blacks and whites in our congregation truly love each other, a beautiful fruit to show forth the Lord's victory for our neighborhood. Antagonists in war even came together as one. Not only Jeanine and Dorothy but J.B. Maw, who had been a naval gunboat commander in Vietnam, and another brother, Chamchan, who had been a Laotian commander and police chief of Vientiane, learned of their brotherhood in Christ. This was in spite of the fact that J.B. had nearly been killed in the heat of battle by Laotian troops he had trained. Perhaps the greatest healing that took place was between the "charismatics" and the "noncharismatics" who both truly enjoy being called Christians together.

In May of 1975, Judy and I and Matt and Donna Steward attended the Fourth International Conference of the Holy Spirit within the Presbyterian and Reformed traditions in Montreat, North Carolina. The Lord taught us all very hard lessons there, particularly concerning submission. We were all on fire when we went but our zeal turned to tears as we listened with our hearts during the four-day conference and then reviewed the tapes on the way home. Everyone at the conference—whether pastor, elder or church member—was admonished, pulled and stretched, edified, entreated, everything short of commanded to go home to their church and grow in submission. Some of the examples we heard, both positive and negative, moved us with conviction in our hearts and we determined to be in total submission as we arrived back in Providence. For all of us it meant offering our lives essentially to the body of elders the Lord had raised up to rule in the congregation. Everything I heard the Lord telling me to do was to go before the elders and the Lord would be faithful through them either in direct confirmations, modifications or flat refusals. In faith He would speak through them concerning all things. Ironically enough Matt was led to ask the conference leadership to pray over him for the gift of wisdom and, as witnessed in the ensuing years, he was abundantly so gifted.

It is that wisdom now which still teaches us and at this point it particularly concerns the whole area of submission. The positive lesson of submission is that it will produce sweet fruit. A Christian properly taught and discipled will welcome the relationship in the body that not only insures him a place but which also is his constant guide, support and truthful sounding board for what he hears the Lord telling him. The sweet fruit develops as we begin to understand that as bond slaves to Christ we are truly set free and that this slavery becomes actualized as we become docile, functioning parts of the body. Submission to authority bridles our innate rebellion, preserves us from making painful mistakes and ultimately affirms our nature in Christ and our sonship in God our Father. Submission by law is operative in every Christian church whether by hierarchy, representative elders or total congregational democracy. It is not insured, however, that it will be led by the Spirit except in radical faith and herein lies seed ground for many problems. Two of the most grievous problems are (1) the authority in a particular church may not have such a radical faith; and (2) those who have submitted can easily do so in a zealous, surrendering experience to later find they too lack the faith or have not dealt with themselves honestly.

Before we left for Montreat, an intercessory prayer group had formed and had already actively prayed for all areas in the church and its work. They had already begun praying for the elders and would gather at the same time the elders met to spend time in prayer. They would then expectantly await word of session decisions. Montreat confirmed that the Lord had led them already into this much-needed vehicle of prayer and concern.

All of this led us to some very important lessons. Some bore immediate fruit and the tree still yields; others were learned after the time for bearing fruit had passed. Let me only mention here some of the outward signs. From the days of first love, fire and zeal until perhaps late 1976 or early 1977 there was faith to sustain growth. Endurance and longsuffering had already begun to develop and we were all hanging in there. But it was also around this time that other evidences began to show a different pattern. The intercessory prayer group stopped meeting. The main prayer meeting began to languish and in 1977 we closed it down. Ironically enough in late 1977 we gave ourselves a spiritual check-up and decided the prognosis was good. As always, there were many things to work on but basically we still saw the Lord's blessing.

In truth, however, the church was again facing a real bench mark time in her growth. I've already mentioned many of the things which were happening to me personally. What I was experiencing and what the church was experiencing will be most clearly seen in the lessons we learned.

What did we learn that's important to share? First, that negativism and hidden resentments that surface to our awareness and then are not shared for whatever reason can deal crippling blows to the work of the Lord in a church. In the first section I spoke of experiences that were meaningful to me in my spiritual pilgrimage both from a positive growth point of view as well as those things the Lord used for correction in my path. In this chapter, I've tried to show what the Lord did among the members of the church. But they and I did not always work in harmony or share the same experiences. This was a difficult hurdle always to overcome and often we were less than truthful with one another. There were times when we allowed things to pass that the Lord took care of and were no longer problems. There were other times, however, when we allowed them to pass and they became buried resentments out of which disharmony would come just at the point of crucial decision-making. At these times, we were not the united body of Christ. Satan worked pretty much at will, unchecked even by faith.

Secondly, we learned, on a much more positive note, that our work in the community which admittedly was begun before the charismatic outpouring was only enhanced and, if anything, infiltrated with more zeal, wisdom and love. Concerning this work we were indeed one in motivation, call and usually in methodology. We moved as one, a witness in itself when there were other areas of concern where we found our oneness in jeopardy. At one point I calculated our involvement in the Capitol Hill Interaction Council and found that some thirty members of our church had volunteered 155 hours per week, equivalent to $20,500 per year at minimum wage—much more than we ever spent on ourselves. This did not include our other direct giving to missions, the fact that others in the congregation were involved in outreach projects other than the Capitol Hill Interaction Council, and that the contribution of many talents of our people into CHIC would be considered more valuable than minimum wage levels. Often the charismatic renewal has been criticized for its lack of concern for neighbors in need and, indeed, I've known a great many persons who were once deeply involved in social action programs who, when touched by the renewal, have hibernated. I've also known why this happened, for their souls were thirsting and the Lord called them out of social concerns for a time of rebuilding. In our case, however, He did not and I believe He truly wants that known. The renewal, baptism in the Holy Spirit, a deepening devotion and love for Jesus, a growing more personal loving relationship with our Father, all of these will ultimately cause our reaching out to our brother to be wiser, more loving and winsome than ever before. It will not, as we are so often criticized for, cause us to withdraw from the world and its concerns. The difference is a joyful, enduring Christian reaching out to the man in the gutter, a Christian who will not withdraw when the going gets rough as opposed to a tired, unrefreshed Christian who will falter in time under the burden of another man in the gutter.

Thirdly, we learned to seek the higher gifts of faith, hope and love. I'm sure it was this seeking that led to the healing of relationships between charismatics and noncharismatics in the congregation. This was to show forth the fruit of the fundamental unity of the movement of the Holy Spirit among our people. Especially did we seek love. I think ironically enough that the fruit of love is very long-term and applies best when patience and endurance and longsuffering have had time enough to work. When one seeks to love, he must almost of necessity learn to hope in things unseen and have faith for miracles; he must ultimately learn humility yet be armored with truth—even bold truth. To go the route of love is the harder route; it is much less flashy and flamboyant, much more demanding of the total self. Again, however, the Lord led us as one to seek this gift. Some of the fruit started to become evident as strangers would visit the church and remark how friendly, warm and genuinely interested the people of the congregation were. We instituted a coffee hour after Sunday worship which was almost as well-attended as worship and ran practically as long. People are hungry for love but they're also hungry to love and the church needs to provide every opportunity it can for the filled cup to be emptied.

There are also some harsher realities. Love is a many-sided gift. It is hard to define. We were led by Father Francis MacNutt in the Atlantic City Conference of 1975 to look at 1 Corinthians 13 in a new light. We were asked to replace the word "love" everywhere it appeared in this chapter with the name of Jesus. That was all right. But then he asked us to replace it with the pronoun "I." He also added the adverb "always" since "love" and "Jesus" synonymously are "always" and absolute. Thus we tried to repeat after Father MacNutt these things, first laughing, then pondering, then stopping.

"I am always patient and kind, I am never jealous or boastful; I am never arrogant or rude. I never insist on my own way; I'm never irritable or resentful; I never rejoice at wrong but I always rejoice in the right. I always bear all things, I always believe all things, I always hope all things, I always endure all things" (paraphrase of 1

Cor. 13:4-7 as offered by Fr. Francis MacNutt).

Paul's definition of love is probably the best anywhere, surpassed only by demonstrations of sacrificing love. The point is that love is never gentle and affectionate without truth. Truth is always much harder to give and to receive than gentleness and we usually tend to rest in the latter. "Truth," Aristotle said, "only hurts when it's supposed to." The truth of love is often disconcerting and disarming. Few of the 17,000 conferees of Atlantic City 1975 could finish repeating all of the thoughts of Paul's definition of love because we had all been convicted by the truth of love. Fr. MacNutt had shared it with us obliquely enough, lovingly enough that the truth was able to penetrate but not pierce the heart. I experienced being convicted and lifted up at the same time.

I had as much difficulty facing the truth, if not more difficulty, than anyone in the congregation. I know from the other side (the side of pride and arrogance) that it takes a very patient, very discerning, almost transparent, always vulnerable love that can then speak truth and strike fire in the heart to make it a heart of flesh. In love we can pretty easily discern another's failings and see where they are headed for danger, but at that point we are in as much danger as they. We may not speak the truth which then leaves both people with only half a cup. Or we may speak the truth out of our own lack of being loved and cause hurt for ourselves and for the other person. To speak the truth in love lovingly is the trick quite far removed from our humanity.

To seek love, the highest gift, is critical to the charismatic movement as well as to all Christian churches, for this gift is the one the Lord has particularly given to be the vehicle toward the unity He is calling for in families, in churches, with His Spirit in the world, and in His body. Jesus gives us a simple clue that we often miss in one of the things He said that is remembered even among non-Christians. He commanded us to love God with all our capacity to love as a response to His first outpouring love for us. Then we hear something very important about the second step in this process. Then Jesus said we must love others as we love ourselves. If we don't love ourselves very much we're not going to be able to love others very much. If we resent ourselves we will pretty easily resent others. We must begin by recognizing our Father's love for us no matter what we do, see what He sees in us and then apply it to ourselves before we can very effectively love anyone else. What if we go one step beyond Father MacNutt's paraphrasing to see ourselves as the object of our own love as defined by Paul? "I am always patient and kind toward myself. I am never jealous toward myself or boastful against myself; I am never arrogant toward myself or rude to myself. I never insist on my own way when it's opposed to myself, I'm never irritable with myself or resentful of myself; I never rejoice at the wrong in me but I always rejoice in the right in me. I always bear all things about myself, I always believe all things in myself, I always hope all things in myself, I always endure all things for myself." It becomes a beautiful lesson of resting in the Spirit as we contemplate that our Father is often much more pleased with us than we are with ourselves. He only asks for a heart that is willing to surrender, a yielding spirit, a little bit of love. He doesn't ask for our works.

Because we did not carefully and pleasingly love ourselves, even from our Father's point of view, we would pick away at each other and inch by inch lose the precious ground the Lord had gained for us and through us toward the end of the unity of His body in the congregation. Hurt would turn to resentment, then to sin and this replaced the seed of healthy self-love with pride.

Fourthly, we learned we had a strong and healthy desire for Christian unity and as we lay ourselves open and vulnerable we were hurt and, unfortunately, never able to fully recover. This stemmed again from our lack of truthfulness, our immaturity in loving, our own resentment that we kept in our hearts at that time. The Lord had given us in our own congregation a people He had drawn together from every varied background and we could not, nor did we ever, conceive of ultimate divisions among Christians. Our everyday life found us constantly in contact with Christians from other churches and we shared all of life together. The streets of Smith Hill then and now are often the scenes of small groups of people praying together and never a word is raised about what church a person attends. When the people were out helping, whether in Capitol Hill Interaction Council or in their many social service jobs, the question of where a person went to church was never raised as a requirement for receiving aid. (I don't mean to suggest that other churches did this either. It was totally foreign for us to think we were anything but brothers and sisters of our one Lord Jesus and all sons and daughters of our Father. So simply had we learned this loving and saving truth that any suggestion of division for any reason became a violation of conscience grave enough to question any scheme or structure that tended in any way to separate the family of God.) We learned to accept that these were the days when the Lord was drawing His body together and His intentions were serious. We welcomed this and believed He had brought together a people who had been prepared since their various childhoods to receive it in a unique community that had been prepared by His Spirit to be a model to the world.

Lastly, our understanding of submission lacked the radical faith on the part of all to follow through. It tended in me as well as others to reinforce our passive natures while in still others it fostered first a reaction of rebellion and then, as time progressed, because there was no agreement on accountability—the opposite of unity—an individualistic free approach to the working out of our Christian faith. Essentially everyone loved the Lord and there were countless times of love shared between and among us but then each one went his separate way and performed ministry as he saw fit. We even joked at one point about how difficult it would be for us to get in the way of the Lord because we had no unified program to trip Him up. Anything that happened was surely Him because we had no concerted plans of our own. The deeper problem is not funny of course. Authority, as mentioned before, comes from Christ and we ought to be in submission to the Lord in each other by the Spirit. Especially where the Lord has given such a yearning desire for the unity of His body ought these principles to operate. To do so obviously means a number of things. Perhaps the first of these is to place our pride in submission to Him and be willing to work through the consequences. Certainly not the least of these is to grow in all the awareness, discernment and wisdom we can. Satan doesn't want the body of Christ together. When the body of Christ is together it means he will be rendered useless. He will no longer be able to stop the healing and evangelization of the world because the unified body of Christ will stand up with authority and summarily dismiss him. As long as he can keep people divided, he wins every inning. Surely if we are to submit to the Lord in each other then we must be discerning and truthful as well as loving when we relate to one another and we all must become acutely aware that the closer we come toward being the body of Christ the angrier our enemy will become. Most churches lack discernment and as long as they do they will only bumble along. That's not what the Lord is calling for today. He is calling for the body to come together; He is calling for the world to be evangelized. There are so many people in the world, especially the young, who are fed with drugs, who worship in pagan or deceptive cults, claiming to be Christian or otherwise, who are spiritually aware and sensitive and searching for truth. Where will the Lord send them for help? Who will He send to help them? Occultists and Satanists know more about Jesus than many Christians. Surely the Lord can't use people who are unaware of the problem or people who don't understand the source of evil to be a help very long to those who are in it. Christian people can be deceived. I was. I know others can be. We live in a world that is becoming increasingly hostile to Christianity. If we do not band together now out of loving desire, we may well find, not long from now, that we must band together out of necessity. Being banded together helps give us the courage we need to follow through on the discernment and awareness the Lord gives us.

Now that the Lord has shown the church how to love without condemnation it is now ready to take the next step to bind the body together, to walk in its God-given faith and take the gates by storm.

Concerning the Trends report, I couldn't agree more that the warmth and love of the congregation is the determining factor for people who are considering becoming part of a local congregation. These are wonderful fruits of the Spirit and they indicate that the people are spiritual. But it must be said alongside that there are many other groupings in the world outside of the Christian church that also display these same fruits. There is still an abiding truth in the Word being preached and heard. The Word is the Church's one offensive weapon. Fruits of the Spirit come from a spiritual world, over which Jesus Christ is victor and those who approach this spiritual world without the Word may well find the fruits but not the Savior. Again, I'm suggesting that if a church body is not aware of this world and its enemy, they may indeed draw others to them through their warmth and love but it will be like the seed falling on shallow soil. It will produce a beautiful plant for a while but then it will die for lack of roots. To suggest, as the Trends report does, that a church's theology or its openness to the new birth in Christ and subsequent baptism in the Spirit are not determining factors in a church's growth or decline abrogates the whole Word. Our church, United Presbyterian, in Providence, sociologically doesn't fit the pattern. The people are born again, they are Spirit-filled, they are also warm, friendly and loving. The numbers continue to go down. One must look beyond a sociological survey for the answers. What makes the church distinctive is that Christ is the Head. Why not then go to the Head of the church for the answers? Why not seek the mind of Christ?

The Challenge of Faith

We forget the promises of God and that is the challenge of faith! He spoke. It is not His fault we forget what He said He would do.

The doorbell rang and I went to answer it to find Reverend John Watkins standing on the porch. It was a quiet Sunday evening and a good time for visitors. I had known John from presbytery as he was one of my brethren who had recently finished a call as assistant pastor in one of our Presbyterian churches, and most recently had been a counselor at the junior college. I didn't know John well but knew him enough to appreciate the strength of his faith and his concerns surrounding Christian community. As John sat down he simply said, "Here I am. Can you use me?" I couldn't believe what I was hearing and it took me the whole evening to accept the fact that John wanted to work with me and our church free of charge, unconditionally, wherever I could use him. I was not accustomed to people asking me how they could help me with such an unconditional faith nor was I expecting the Lord, at this point in time, to fulfill a promise He had made to me in the first days of our experience with the Holy Spirit—that He would send other ministers of the Word to help in the cause of Christian unity in our community. I had forgotten His promise. John was such a precious gift that I just melted again before my Lord for His faithfulness and love. John and I were to learn together a very real hand-glove relationship and when I resigned, John was appointed interim pastor for the congregation who by now loved him and needed him.

During our time together John moved into the neighborhood, bought a home for himself and his new bride, Anita, and became a very uplifting part of all our lives. John now preaches to perhaps thirty people on any given Sunday. After worship the people go home instead of staying for the fellowship hour because the fellowship hour is no longer a reality. John's faith is still strong.

The Lord promised He would fill the church, that it would be a dynamic, vibrant light and witness to Him, that many would come with needs to be met but therein would they find the loving, affectionate hand of our Lord reaching out to them.

Some years ago the word was to hang in, endure, grow in patience and understanding. Many churches have learned that lesson at least sufficient for the day. Now I believe the word is a different one. "Now churches, rise up. Accept your resurrection. Live in a radical faith. Band together in truth, wisdom and discernment. You have all the gifts you need. Be courageous and follow the Spirit. Let no tradition or enemy, visible or invisible, stop you. You are being prepared for battle. Strip down. Exercise the authority I have given you. Draw yourselves together. Claim the victory of my Son on the cross and from the empty tomb. Determine to walk in life and not death. The victory is won. It is only for you to listen to my Spirit and obey, for the sealed orders are opened. Expect a hostile world but know I go before you with my mighty arm. Be willing to go where you have not gone before. Be willing to go beyond your experience. Others were called before you. Many have not listened. The time is short but it is not too late. I will yet raise up a people who will follow. Open your ears and hear what the Spirit and the Word have to say! I will yet build a witness to my love and victory!"

Dear Lord, you know what lies ahead and you know the hearts of your people. Prepare us all as you must; please give us eyes to see and ears to hear. We are afraid so many times, Father. Forgive us for forgetting how very much you love us. Forgive us for not remembering the cross. Forgive us for our faithlessness. We are weak and our clay feet don't move. Restore within us a right spirit that we as your church may still be a witness to your love and victory. Lead us into unity as your body. Wash away the bitter gall of our sin.

Father, I pray you would visit once again the reign of your Spirit upon the United Presbyterian Church on Chalkstone Avenue and all churches like her and fulfill your promises of long ago that you would raise up a people who would be a light to the nations. I pray in the name of my Lord Jesus. Amen.

8

Relationships with Other Church Bodies

If then God gave the same gift to them as he gave to us when we believed in the Lord Jesus Christ, who was I that I could withstand God? (Acts 11:17)

The United Baptist Church and Us

None of us has more or less struggle than Peter had as the Lord counseled him through a vision to cross over traditional understandings to new pathways of our God. Cornelius is pictured as much more eager for this meeting than Peter was but there may well have been fears on his part, too. Jesus chose twelve very different men to walk more closely with Him than we can sometimes fathom. It's difficult for us to imagine that bringing them to unity of purpose had its own strains. When churches agree to work together toward certain selected purposes, many fears also emerge that would otherwise lay dormant. Unless these fears can be dealt with openly and honestly they will present an undercurrent of potential resentment and bitterness that leads to the destruction of common purpose, however lofty and scriptural it may be. Rev. Edwin Thornton spoke briefly at a dinner the church gave us on the day of my effective resignation saying simply that he and I and others in our two churches had labored hard on an idea that had not yet reached its time. Ed was used to this happening in his over forty years of ministry, watching churches accept a decade or generation later the first movements of the Spirit mentioned years earlier. He had also watched the pain of loneliness and separation for those who tried to walk abreast of the Spirit's promptings, as they were sometimes seen as unwise or out of step by the majority of people. I was comforted by his comments, for they were an affirmation of what I knew we both believed at one time—that it was not only the Lord's will for our churches to be together but it was also unthinkable for them to remain apart.

Ed and I had first met through Nancy Rougvie, member of the United Baptist pulpit committee that had called Ed to be their new pastor. By then she had become a dear friend of Judy and me. (Nancy has been and continues to be a deep blessing to us. Ever since I can remember she has carried a special burden in her heart for us and has given so unselfishly of her time to us that she really is a part of our family. For many years Nancy would come over and baby-sit with our children free of charge so Judy and I could get out for a while and appreciate other surroundings. Her heart has been so willing that we have only appreciated her as a gift and have never been made to feel we have burdened her. This is such a help to a pastor's family that I mention it here so that anyone in a church who might feel the same calling for their pastor and his family would be encouraged to go and offer. Tom and Valerie Carleton and Madeline Tramantano have been the same kind of blessing to us because they realized we were people just like anyone else who needed love and friendship. And also I want to encourage any pastors, pastors' wives or pastors' children reading this to not feel guilty if you have a friend or two within the congregation. The Lord would seek to bless you in this way without worry of jealousy or envy on the part of people in your congregation. He knows as none other the burdens you carry and the faithfulness to your call you exhibit seven days a week. He will not begrudge you a friend and this is not to say He is still not your best friend. He knows our needs and rejoices when we accept the gifts He offers.)

Prior to Ed's coming, I had met weekly with Rev. Roger Pruitt who was United's pastor when I came, and Rev. Charles Haines, pastor of the Mount Pleasant Baptist Church. United was a block away from our church; Mt. Pleasant was about a mile away. We had progressed far enough in our relationships that the United

Baptist pulpit committee wanted Chuck and me to meet Ed to see if we could work with him before they issued the final call. We were elated to find Ed receptive to answering the call of United Baptist Church specifically for the reason of bringing our churches together. It would be his last pastorate and mission of the Lord as he planned even then to retire from this church. In August of 1978 he did indeed effect his retirement. As we met in Ed's hotel room for the first time, Chuck and I were thrilled. Nancy knew we would be because they had picked Ed because of his desire to work with us and lead them into union.

As we grew in fellowship together we began to lay out the framework for our churches working together. Ed and I were already active in the Capitol Hill Interaction Council in which a great number of people from both of our churches found themselves participating. We finally presented papers to our respective ruling bodies (which they had authorized us to design) outlining the working relationship for our churches' cooperative efforts. We had borrowed a considerable amount of material from the design put forth by the Consultation on Church Union, a body of churchmen brought together after a 1961 conference in San Francisco between Bishop James Pike, an Episcopalian, and Eugene Carson Blake, the Stated Clerk of the United Presbyterian General Assembly. By the time we borrowed material from the consultation's suggested design for cooperative union there were fully ten mainline Protestant denominations involved in the consultation, of which both the American Baptists and United Presbyterians were a part. In our design we suggested a parish council consisting of six members from each church totaling eighteen people with the three pastors serving as ex-officio members. Appropriate committees were set up for coordinating concerns of fellowship, Christian education, future planning and design, mission, etc. The design papers were then presented to the individual church's ruling bodies, were accepted without exception and we were off and running on what appeared to be a significant forward thrust for all of our churches. Church schools of the United Baptist and United Presbyterian churches were merged with one joint treasury and curriculum. Monthly fellowship nights brought together the congregations of all three churches. Cluster study meetings in homes of members of the three churches saw successful Lenten programs each year. Maundy Thursday and Christmas Eve Communion services brought us all together for the sacrament. Mission together consisted of our joint efforts through the Capitol Hill Interaction Council. Worship services during the summer were combined to allow for the pastors and organists of each church to go on vacation without employing substitutes as well as to bring our people together for consistent combined worship. A children's choir was begun with children from both the churches in Smith Hill as well as some of the neighborhood children. They and various groupings of the choir were good enough to finally cut a record and to perform several times a year for a variety of church occasions all over the Northeast. Significant decisions of the parish council required a ratifying vote by each of the church's separate ruling bodies before implementation could take place. A week night Bible study and prayer meeting began especially for members of the United Presbyterian and United Baptist churches.

The American Baptist Convention of Rhode Island and Providence Presbytery of the Synod of New England were kept fully informed of each step we made together and both higher judicatories were supportive and encouraging. As we progressed and gained momentum in our work together it became apparent to many of those involved that we had reached the point of taking the next step toward initiating discussion of organic union. The parish council suggested to each of the three churches that they be empowered to pursue study of organic union. The council awaited a reply. Mt. Pleasant Baptist Church voted down the proposal and withdrew from the parish council. Shortly after this, Rev. Haines resigned his pastorate, feeling that his work toward unity was at cross purposes with the basic desire of his congregation. (Ironically, the next pastor of the Mt. Pleasant Baptist Church was a United Presbyterian.) United Baptist and United Presbyterian both voted yes and a design committee was set up to develop the design that would bring our two churches together into one church. Care was taken in selecting the committee in that all voices would be adequately represented. We searched out material from other recent organic unions where Baptist and Presbyterian churches were involved and studied our own particular needs, as well as our denominational guidebooks. A design was set that met the requirements of both judicial systems with particular emphasis placed upon the fact that membership in either denomination would be preserved. A new member could join either of the two representative denominations or now a new body made up of the church congregation by itself. Any pastor called would be a member of both denominations. Initial approvals were set by denominational representatives. Meetings of explanation and preparation gave opportunity for questions from the members of the congregations. These were held informally after suppers. The questions and comments led to the fleshing out of the design. The first proposed step came from the parish council to be ratified by the ruling boards. It involved monthly combined worship services in alternating churches much as we did in the summer for convenience. This time we would be combining services during the winter when there was no such reason. These monthly worship services would afford us all the pleasure of hearing the children's choir which normally could not happen with separate worship services and would also serve to point out our unity in Christ with no other motive. We would simply worship Him together. Little things had happened along the way which opened hearts. The Baptist church, not a creedal church, easily joined with us as we recited together the Apostles' Creed each week during summer worship. Before Chuck had left Mt. Pleasant Baptist, he baptized our infant son, Ken. The list of exciting experiences could go on. We truly shared our lives together.

The Diaconate of the Baptist Church took the proposal of the initial step suggested by the parish council to a congregational meeting where it won unanimous approval. The session of elders of the Presbyterian church did the same, suggesting approval. Though it was not ecclesiastically necessary, it was felt that the step was significant enough to have the congregation voice its desire. The vote to proceed carried only by a slight majority accompanied by threats from a few of the dissenters that they would leave the church should the eventuality of the combined worship services take place.

This was a deep wound to the heart and, though it was not lethal, we still have not fully recovered from it. Vital signs quickly showed a decline. The six Presbyterians, mostly active elders, on the parish council lost authority, zeal and forward momentum. I was stunned and after the initial shock set about trying to build bridges—but we were to never regain the vision.

The parish council still meets but now only perfunctorily. Combined summer worship has been maintained but basically for its obvious practicality. The Bible study/prayer meeting continued until the felt need for a separate prayer meeting employing the gifts arose in the Presbyterian church. The papers that had been labored over for so long were never again presented to any committee or board for consideration. Maundy Thursday and Christmas Eve are still beautiful times of sharing. Ed and I stopped meeting though we still worked together in the Capitol Hill Interaction Council and in other projects.

The dismantling process was confusing because we still held on to the initial commitment that we felt was the Lord's call to be together while at the same time our very togetherness promised a certain fruitlessness if we could not likewise pursue deeper organic union. Finally we severed ourselves from one another and began separate programs that we had previously enjoyed together. Last year the final support system was removed as we initiated separate church schools and divided equally the last offerings between the two schools. What was once envisioned to be a strong combined Protestant witness to build further unity with our Catholic brothers and sisters has now once again fallen into a fractured witness at best with two struggling small Protestant congregations, only one block apart.

What went wrong? Where does the fault lie? Did we wrongly hear the Lord? Had we not sufficiently mended our own fences before we ventured to covenant across them? There are probably as many different answers as there are different traditions and as much as I struggled then and more peacefully meditate now on these answers I confess I do not know the reason for failure. I do know this, however, that the Lord continues to grieve over our brokenness, that He continually presents unifying challenges to all segments and structures of the Christian body whether husband and wife or church denominations, that He does not force union upon us any more than He forces himself and that as sweet as Christian people can be they can also fail on their end of the covenant. They can easily make wrong choices. He always leaves the decision with us but what baffles me the most is this: I have found so many times with the Lord that though He leaves the decision with me and never forces me to decide according to His will or direction, He also provides my heart with a yearning desire to join with Him in oneness whether in terms of my own salvation, a step of righteousness, the oneness of His body or other goals. He has given me this desire particularly for unity of His body and I'm bewildered that so few other Christians seem to care or that so many who are indeed precious in the Lord can so easily allow their traditions to take precedence over the oneness of today's Christian family.

If I had it all to do over again, the only thing I would perhaps have done differently would be to remind the people of my church that though the vote was uncomfortably close, we did indeed vote yes by 51 percent and that uniting with the Baptists should be our direction. Let your yes be yes and your no be no so the Lord can then continue to work.

As the Lord would have it, however, we were soon to find another challenge at our door with even more variables to deal with.

St. Patrick's Roman Catholic Church and Us

I've already indicated the ever-deepening relationships between several members and the pastoral team of St. Patrick's with Judy and myself. This now involves a growing number of the members of our Presbyterian church as well. If there was a transition that could be marked in the mind of the Lord as we embarked on this adventure with St. Patrick's, having come away from discouragement and failure with United Baptist, it is perhaps the same transition we find in Paul as he recounts his spiritual journey in Romans. In Romans 7 he tells us of himself as a renewed man under the law but still ignorant of the delivering power of the Holy Spirit. In Romans 8 we see him delivered from law, able to walk even more fully in Spirit than law, and therefore, no longer condemned by his own flesh. We pursued union with the Baptists because it was righteous, it was the will of God generally and because anything less than this pursuit would be ludicrous. We discovered, however, that we were on different spiritual wavelengths as we began to experience the releasing power of the Holy Spirit and they did not. We were still Christian brothers and sisters in the same family of God but with ever-widening differences in perception. What was happening to us in the Presbyterian church brought us into immediate oneness with the people in the Word of God Community at St. Patrick's. Yet a deeper paradox arose in that many of our older members had worked all their lives alongside the older members of United Baptist in the shops and factories. They already had a natural bonding when we began fellowshiping as church congregations. There was little if any of this with people in St. Patrick's as most of the Word of God Community had been transplanted from other parts of the state and the part of our congregation responsive to the outpouring of the Spirit was not indigenous to the community either. We were, for all intents and purposes, one day strangers, the next day brothers and sisters with a phenomenal common bond and heritage. It seemed in the beginning that nothing would be impossible as we grew together in Romans 8 life. There was never much talk about structure—only the pure unadulterated joy of being together whenever we could. It also seems true that the need for more frequent fellowship and sharing is much greater in those who experience this walk in the Spirit than the corresponding need in those who don't experience the same workings of the Spirit. This led us to even greater expectations of unity in the body of Christ than we had experienced before and our prayers grew in fervor and our claims of faith grew in magnitude.

Our greatest attempts at structuring our lives together have come through the Capitol Hill Interaction Council as well as other programs which have emerged directly from a group of Spirit-filled Christians from our two churches sitting down together, praying, hearing the Lord and then proceeding with His direction. They have all ended up including a much larger body and serving a much greater need than anything our churches might, normally speaking, do together. We never pursued structural unity except at the level of combining our separate prayer meetings or perhaps beginning a new venture of healing services together. The desire to do this was strong, but in actuality we were speaking of putting together twenty people from our prayer meeting (many of whom were Catholic) with 500 people of St. Patrick's prayer meeting, and somehow the practicality of this overcame our faith in the healed one body of Christ. It was like joining the little toe to the whole body and it simply required super-abundant faith to proceed with the thought that the whole world would see the one body of Christ now in this prayer meeting and thereby be evangelized. The little toe never really grew enough to even peek out of the shoe and say, "Here I am." In the meetings mentioned above where we would come together, it would always mean 50 percent of our body meeting with only 2 percent of St. Patrick's to even achieve balance.

There were some failures in these smaller groupings I would like to mention and then go on to briefly discuss the still-unique and paradoxical witness of our two renewing parishes working together. The failures are significant in that they're always a little bewildering and raise questions on the one hand, while they point out the clear fact that the Lord works through frail and fallible earthen vessels on the other hand to accomplish His purposes. Though we are always called to share faith and make a positive confession, that is more the attitude, perspective or centrality out of which we must deal with the whole and full truth. Though there is always victory in the Lord, we must, in the context of that victory, realize that sometimes people we pray with for healing are not healed, that sometimes programs initiated in the Spirit are not successful, that all we do as Spirit-filled Christians is not of the Lord—and yet we still know, paradoxically, that the Lord is in control.

With fairly equal representation from our two churches we met on numerous occasions to pursue a number of visions the Lord had given to several of us. Out of these numerous occasions, four of the times we came together resulted in failure.

One time we gathered for a meeting for the purpose of beginning either a restaurant or soup kitchen. About twenty-five people came to pray and discuss, for they all had some part of a vision for this to happen. The Lord was calling for it and this meeting was in faithful response. By the time the meeting closed there was no need to come together again, for we all knew it wouldn't take place.

Much more disconcerting was the series of times when we prayed together for the implementation of an ecumenical, charismatic high school. Seldom was I ever involved in a series of meetings that was so thoroughly guided by the Lord and led prophetically every step of the way. The Lord was clearly promising the school—it was only for us to ask and He would provide all the blueprints. During this series of meetings educators from a three-state radius were involved. Some fifty people were active and committed at various levels, design papers were drawn up, dates had been projected, tasks were assigned. Then, almost as quickly as it had started, it stopped. Everyone who had been a part of these meetings had often witnessed to the faithfulness of the Lord as He led us, to the overwhelming sense of vision and purpose, to the incredible way in which each step forward together was blessed by the blueprint answers. It was as if we were ballooning with steady-paced winds, making solid progress only to ride into a calm and suddenly drop to earth before we ever realized what happened.

The next series of meetings still concerned our youth as we attempted to bring together all the young people of our churches in a fellowship program. This program was begun out of raw need, supported by parents, young people, and churches. It had progressed to the point of actual programs and participation. All the successful tools we had all learned through previous experiences were used. All was set in motion, everyone was pleased and fulfilled but again it stopped overnight.

The final failure and perhaps the most significant was when we voted as a session of ruling elders to meet with the pastoral team of St. Patrick's and they likewise decided to meet with us—but we never did.

There are many deterrents to Christians trying to come together: our human pride, jealousy, envy, resentment or the ugly meaningless traditions of our structures, the return to law when we've been delivered by the Holy Spirit of God from law and the ugliest of all, Satan himself. Satan doesn't want the body of Christ together, he doesn't want our young people living in a supportive community of faith from their peers, he doesn't want the ruling bodies of congregations to even look at each other with loving eyes.

I mentioned that the whole truth must be set in the context of the Lord's victory. He never leaves us desolate. He began the Food Cooperative. He has provided all these young people with parents whom He still continues to set free in love. He still blesses all our churches and has found other ways of bringing our church shepherds and leaders together.

Perhaps most significantly, however, He has allowed us to grow up together, to fellowship and share and work in hundreds of little ways, to heal our resentments and hurts through the failures, to be structured together or not, and to grow in our desire to be one with each other. Because we never suggested structuring our churches together the Lord has allowed us to experience a beautiful unity and oneness outside of structure that's totally real and which for all intents and purposes is ready for His next step. We work together hand in hand six days a week. We eat in one another's homes from one table potentially six days a week. Paradoxically, on the seventh day the structure and tradition of our churches prevents us from being together and in that pain we grow even more in our desire to bring together the body of Christ. That's the positive witness even amidst the failures—that we are the one body of Christ and by our very real oneness we both call the structures to truth and prepare for the day when there may be no church structures as we know them today. In the mystery of the Lord, we've never heard Him say, "Come out of your churches." Indeed, we have heard the opposite. Alongside of this, however, He has given us the Christian family outside of our churches. This is oftentimes more meaningful to us than that within. He calls us to meet together as often as we possibly can with Christians of all backgrounds and traditions in open demonstrations of His one body as well as gifts of the Holy Spirit. Paradoxically, He also calls us to surrender to Him and each other in our own churches. The positive witness of United Presbyterian and St. Patrick's is that we've done just that. We await, as we're called to repentance over the broken body, for these days are only days of transition and preparedness for the coming new age when there will be only one body of Christ. Praise God! And the world will see the arising of all the sons of God together. In still another way the Lord led us (United Baptist, St. Patrick's, United Presbyterian) to prepare. It surrounds the holiday of Thanksgiving.

Thanksgiving

Thanksgiving is perhaps the most wonderful time of year in Smith Hill. It is the most visible occasion of total Christian unity we celebrate. All the churches, described in chapter 10, gather two nights before Thanksgiving Day to worship in praise and thanksgiving. Each year a different pastor brings the message, combined choirs sing, men and women from each church as well as the Capitol Hill Interaction Council participate in the planning and leadership of the evening. Each year a different church hosts the evening and prepares a fellowship hour to follow. All the people bring food and canned goods as well as money donations for the remaining work that is planned for the rest of the week. Each year provides memorable scenes and joyful experiences because the spirit of the occasion has always been so exciting and the fellowship almost explosive. The charged atmosphere of the evening gives each participant a small glimpse of the glory of heaven. We leave knowing that we have been in a very special place and time of our Lord's visitation.

The next day we gather again in small teams to distribute food and food vouchers provided through the collection of the previous evening. Some years we have purchased turkeys for distribution; other years the vouchers have been redeemable in local markets.

More recently the vouchers come from Our Daily Bread Food Cooperative and they are usually large enough to purchase a turkey. Along with the bags of food, a Bible is often placed in the bag too. The teams delivering have always sustained the joy from the previous evening and their smiling, joyful faces have always done as much as the bag of groceries they hand to the poor families. Countless times there are tears on the part of both the giver and the receiver. This part of our Thanksgiving celebration is repeated at Christmas too and between the two occasions, over 400 families receive over $4,000 worth of food and priceless good will.

There is still joy left over from our Tuesday evening service after Wednesday, and thanks giving doesn't end there. Particularly a ministry of St. Patrick's, but one open to all who care to join, are massive Thanksgiving Day and Christmas Day meals for all in the entire city of Providence who might be alone or stranded on those days. Many families come bringing a meal they cooked at home to share with any other person who comes. There are always trays and bins filled with more food so that everyone who comes will be fed and many leave with an extra bag of food under their arms. To ensure that no one is missed a coordinated caravan of cars and trucks and mini buses goes out mid-morning of the holiday to all the hotels, bars, street corners, bus and train stations, anywhere a person alone might be, and people are brought back literally by the hundreds to share in this day of great joy and thanksgiving. Again, several thousand dollars are spent but this time the sum is used to feed well over 1,000 people each time it happens. From sunup to sundown people work and there has not been one time of this sharing when some of the people who come don't accept Jesus into their lives for the first time. Not a few then become an ongoing care and concern—especially for the social work ministry of St. Patrick's.

There are some other results from our work together on the Hill. Each year, two weeks before Christmas, the Capitol Hill Interaction Council sponsors a used toy sale, from toys gathered up all year, where parents can buy good used toys between a range of twenty-five cents to two dollars. Each year they have a selection of over 10,000 toys to choose from. Adjacent to the toy sale room (which is in St. Patrick's gym), there is another smaller room, where children may buy presents, all priced at twenty-five cents, for their parents from donations throughout the year from adults. The money collected from this sale is used to provide the Christmas Day meal and food distribution.

Another magnificent, uplifting day is witnessed on the third Saturday of September each year when the Butterfly Handcrafts Shop sponsors a festival in St. Patrick's parking lot. All of the Capitol Hill Interaction Council bustles, the churches stream out, thousands of people gather to hear festive music and speeches. There are drum corps concerts, clowns, vendors, crafts tables, family yard sales, politicians, barefoot kids, bishops and priests, a ten-cent cup of coffee. I know this day each year is a witness to the Lord, for during one of them I came to know the gentle touch of the Holy Spirit.

On Easter morning at sunrise we also gather together to celebrate the risen Lord at the busiest intersection of main streets on the Hill. In front of the Capitol Hill Interaction Council's building at a place where thousands of cars pass each day we lift up our hands in praise, knowing the glory of our Lord, and consecrating this place as holy ground, ground where our risen Lord walks each day through the din of traffic, the shouts of people, the silent hurts and pains of the hearts of His poor. But on this hushed morning when all the world turns its heart toward an empty tomb, Jesus walks in the triumphant song of His people. After worshiping together here we then walk one block to either the Presbyterian church or the Baptist church for a pancake breakfast sponsored by the parish council.

Though all of the above are one-day events, they powerfully show forth the lofty and mighty power of our Lord as we gather together. They could not happen without the steady work of His Spirit and His people every other day of the year. They are like the wise and mature old man who can rest in his wisdom because it is built on many days of toil and heartbreak, many days of growing and sharing, many days of forgiveness and love.

Father, you have called us to a task that many times seems impossible for our minds to grasp. Though all of our hearts can be given to you in sweet communion and our lives surrendered as completely as we know how; though we praise you together and confess in full and positive faith our love for you and for each other—there are still many voices. Surely, in you there is no division or failure, yet within our humanity we cannot fully grasp your perfect love and unity. Father, please forgive us again and please do not remove from us the yearning for oneness with you and each other. Continue to show us a yet more perfect way.

Father, I look upon Jesus as He gives up His life and I see His humanity and love. I know I'm supposed to only make a positive confession before you and my brothers and sisters, but I also know I have failed as I look upon Him. My heart breaks for every time I have not loved with His love and for all the times my pride stood in the way. Father, forgive me, humble me, help me to cast out my fears with your perfect love. Please let my heart flow with Your Spirit within to say, simply, "I love you." Amen.

9

Relationships with the Larger Body

By this we may be sure that we are in him: he who says he abides in him ought to walk in the same way in which he walked. (1 John 2:5-6)

Because of the fellowship and love that had been shared in the various relationships previously mentioned, other persons were drawn into the same sense of vision that was beginning to develop among us—Christians banded together doing the simple things of sharing life, praising God while seeking out His will, and being faithful together in the things God called us to and which were right before us. This was exactly the place He desired us to be in His plan of historic salvation for today and we knew He would bless with a double portion everything we attempted together in His name. This experience had already been confirmed countless times as people from our church and St. Patrick's would come together whether in prayer or in helping the poor—whatever. The basis for our coming together was the unity we already felt through the work of the Holy Spirit leading us directly to Jesus our Lord, and to His Word, very definitely the guiding tool for all of us—Catholic and Protestant alike. (I remember as a child growing up in the United Presbyterian Church often hearing the criticism of our Roman Catholic brothers and sisters that they did not know the Word, have access to it, or much less use it authoritatively. How surprised I was to even remember that early prejudice in the midst of a prayer meeting at St. Patrick's where hundreds of Roman Catholic Christians were carrying worn-out, marked-up Bibles, quoting from them as they shared what the Lord had been saying to them during the previous week and so obviously thirsting for the Word even during the prayer meeting. It strikes me that the Westminster Confession could have been written at any one of these prayer meetings but, greater than that, the Holy Spirit has, overnight, wiped away centuries of division and we can rejoice.)

It became increasingly clear to us that great strides in evangelism would be made in just the few short years ahead. As already evidenced, when we found ourselves sharing the Lord together with someone who did not know Him, as we marched out together in unity the criticism that the world has always leveled at the church no longer held sway in preventing a person from accepting Christ. It also became clear that, indeed—as Christians stood together simply praising God—the walls of the world's and Satan's opposition would crumble when confronted with the light of our Lord Jesus. And so it was that we began to invite especially the shepherds, the pastors and priests, who were beginning to sense some of the same vision, to meet with us and await what might develop. We never really named ourselves until the fall of 1978 when we became affiliated with the world-wide group called simply "John 17:21." For present purposes I will call us "The Wednesday Morning Group" out of which came much of what follows. Even to this day, though small in number, I believe it will be a most significant group in the future of Christianity in Rhode Island.

The Wednesday Morning Group

Jake and Matt and I had for many years spoken of our desire to bring together the pastors and priests of the various Spirit-filled congregations in the state for the possible coordination of our work, for prayer and healing services, for fellowship—or for whatever purpose the Lord might show us. This was the impetus for what has become the Wednesday Morning Group (John 17:21) and, although other things we often dreamed of doing together never went beyond the talking stage, this was one idea we committed to follow through on and did. We invited who we knew and had fellowshiped with in the past through other organizations and discovered a listing of over forty men. The group has never seen this many in a meeting, but it has included as many as twenty at given times and usually there are six or eight in attendance. There are some regulars who seldom miss and I would like to list them with their denominational affiliation so there is a sense of who we are in tradition:

Rev. Ken Steigler, United Methodist pastor
Rev. Andy LePenta, United Methodist pastor
Rev. Aaron Usher, Episcopal priest
Rev. Robert Hargreaves, Episcopal priest
Rev. Tim Gillen, Roman Catholic priest
Rev. Donald Kopenen, American Lutheran pastor
Rev. John Cooper, Assemblies of God pastor
Rev. Bob Salliby, Assemblies of God pastor
Mr. Philip Sheridan, nondenominational layman, Bible teacher
and shepherd of "We Would See JESUS" ministries
Also Judy often attends our meetings.

We began by learning more about each other and the work we were engaged in, and we prayed together. We've always found an unspeakable joy in our prayer life together. Sometimes we begin the meeting with prayer; usually it comes in the middle and starts only at one person's suggestion. Occasionally, we've waited too long before we start and men have to leave but nonetheless they leave feeling refreshed for having had the fellowship, the sharing of visions, the support and upbuilding of genuine Christian love. In most meetings I have attended with clergy I would always become aware of the competitiveness, the envy and strife, the gamesmanship, the hypocrisy—the ugliness of our humanity. This was never a part of the Wednesday morning meetings which were conversely very mutually supportive and threaded through with gentle, genuine love. Trust levels were high enough in the beginning that we could share pretty honestly without fear of rejection or that we would take on a lesser role of significance. Out of this has also come a greater appreciation of what it means to be a servant of the Lord—shepherd and prophet, pastor and priest—in the sense of the Lord's tremendous outpouring love and constant concern for His servants. The beauty of this experience and the truthful, genuine, loving nature of our relationships within this group are most definitely a fruit of the baptism in the Spirit we all shared and the centrality of Jesus in our midst to which the baptism had led us. The help this kind of group can offer, especially to Christian pastors, is invaluable. Not the least valuable help is the dynamic of honing in clearly on the vision the Lord is giving in a natural setting of accountability and responsibility free of the nonloving restrictions so often found in the structural accountabilities of the church. The church has always held out this ideal of spiritual movement but seldom sees it happen because the structures are equally built upon human frailties. It's a constant joy to be part of a group—truly a rare gift—that can move unhindered with the promptings of the Spirit and learn as the Spirit would teach.

As we settled in to hear what the Lord would have us be about, it became increasingly clear that His desire was for us to visibly demonstrate our unity and the unity of all the Christians in the state. We were also beginning to pick up on a vast healing ministry that would reach out to all people without regard to the nature of their illnesses or the backgrounds out of which they came. We proceeded to follow these two major areas of thinking and soon our meetings became more pointed and purposeful.

As we sought the Lord concerning our visibility as Christians unified to lift Him up, His plan centered in a gathering to His praise and glory, wherein music and hands would be lifted up, voices sharing in unison a loud hosanna and hearts together open to His Spirit. We knew He would pour out His healing love in ways yet undreamed. And so it was that April 17, 1977, became "A Night for Celebration of Our Risen Lord." This was two weeks following Easter and the largest ecumenical gathering of Christians in the recent history of the state of Rhode Island (until May of 1978 when we all came together again). It was on this night at Rhodes-on-the-Pawtuxet that we announced what He had been leading us to in terms of healing ministries and witnessed for the first time, this night, His healing arm through the Christian Professionals.

The vision He gave us concerning healing was an all-inclusive healing ministry that would incorporate, as well as be supportive of, His primary healers in our society—medical doctors, nurses and adjunct fields. Though it took us considerable time to understand this vision and our role in it, we began by inviting two Christian doctors to meet with us and respond to what we were hearing from the Lord. Dr. George Coleman, cancer surgeon and then President of the Rhode Island Medical Association, and Dr. Alvin Gendreau, gynecologist and obstetrician. They met with us separately but said essentially the same things. They cautioned us not to set ourselves apart from or in any way opposite to the medical professions. They told us that doctors in the state were open to the concepts of spiritual healing that we were being shown in the charismatic movement and, paradoxically, they were very skeptical of the charismatic-pentecostal approach to healing which they often experienced in patients' refusals of their physicians' care or prescribed medication once they had experienced the Lord's healing. This was because many patients frequently returned sometime later with conditions that had worsened. Both Dr. Coleman and Dr. Gendreau helped us through these first stages of thought as we took a rather hard look at the situation and our own sense of faith in the Lord's healing gifts. It wasn't long before we recognized the need and call for a separate, ongoing meeting with medical professionals of which we ultimately became a part rather than they becoming a part of us. By the time Rhodes-on-the-Pawtuxet was at hand, they were ready to be an integral part of what happened and that night gave birth to a solidarity within the healing call both of the Lord and the profession to name themselves the Christian Professionals and take their place in the future of the healing arts in Rhode Island.

Rhodes-on-the-Pawtuxet

We couldn't have asked for more pleasant weather as we gathered at Rhodes with the sun beginning to set over what had been a favorite dance hall in the state and a place where thousands of Rhode Island courtships and romances had begun in the days of the big swing bands. The building had fallen into some disrepair and, because of financial reverses, this was to be her last night open. The whole place glistened as the sun went down over the picturesque lake in front of the hall. This was indeed the Lord's night and we were prepared to celebrate it.

The Wednesday Morning Group which was sponsoring the evening had decided fairly early to ask local people to have the various speaking and leadership responsibilities rather than inviting larger names outside of Rhode Island. And so it was that we used ourselves and a few people from outside our group for witnessing. Jake would be the emcee, Aaron would lead in prayers of inner healing; John Polce would be responsible for music; Don Kopenen would sing; Bob Hargreaves would sing and play the guitar in a song the Lord had given him for this night; Ken and Tim would remain in constant intercession and I would announce the Christian Professionals. We sought two witnesses from the state who would most accurately share about this unity that was taking place and the Lord astounded us by a greater witness to unity than we had even dreamed of (as He promised He would) through the sharing of the two people He had chosen. Because we were embarking on a new phase of healing and had been meeting now on several occasions with Dr. Gendreau, it seemed more than fitting that he be asked to speak. His spoken witness, an eloquent, learned and compassionate message on the theology of healing in the new day formed a magnificent and beautiful bridge between the charismatic-pentecostal healing gifts and the profession of medicine. Dr. Gendreau's unspoken witness was his personality and life—a very humble and loving Christian doctor, competent and respected in his profession but also a man who prays with his patients when they're willing, prays for them in any case and always finds some way to share our Lord as they both seek recovery. The second witness for the evening came from a continual word the Lord had shared with us concerning the restoration of the life of His people through the joint efforts of the religious and political communities. Rhode Island is a very fortunate state in many ways, not the least of which is the homogeneity of its people due to its size. Rhode Island, smallest of the Union, is in reality a city-state and, although fraught with many problems, those problems are somehow more manageable and the people can feel a real sense of participatory democracy. It is not uncommon to personally know your governor, senators, congressmen and mayors as well as your city and town councilmen and state representatives to the legislature. As the Lord would have it, we do indeed know these people and especially, for our evening at Rhodes, the governor's wife, Mrs. Marguarite Garrahy. She too agreed to attend; in individual prayer she had received the same scriptural passages and injunctions we did. She shared her witness beautifully and humbly about the Lord's unifying restoration with the political and religious hands clasped together.

Beyond our wildest imaginations the Lord spoke to us of the healing of entire communities and structures in the state—the church itself healed toward a deeper realistic ecumenism, the religious-political-medical structures in the state working hand in hand for the greater life and potential of her people. Old resentments and divisions again were washed away and we found it a joy to pray for one another and lift each other up all as the Lord's anointed to do His will.

Later on in the evening, after the witnessing, corporate praise and song, we had opportunity for individual prayer and I found myself praying on a team with Dr. Gendreau and one of the nurses then drawn to be a part of the Christian Professionals that evening. It was then that I was to witness people some sixty years of age and more, coming for prayer to our team (which was one of perhaps fifteen teams) who had not been to a doctor in over thirty years because they had been hurt and had allowed resentments to become greater than the physical pain they were feeling. Another team of four young men, all bearded and wearing dungarees, all friends of ours called to street evangelism and very much looking the part this night at Rhodes, attracted, for some reason, all ages for prayer and, unlike any other team, merely touched the people, and the objects of their prayers were all slain in the power of the Spirit, one right after another. In no other team did this happen. Yet in other teams people wept and were humbled before the powerful healing arm of the Lord. Hundreds were prayed for and we entered a new page of history in the book of unity.

The Christian Professionals

Grateful to the Lord for the early cautions of Drs. Coleman and Gendreau, the first meetings of the medical group, as we called it then, began with an attitude of inclusion and thankfulness for those who had dedicated their lives to the healing profession. Because all those who attended these first meetings were also recipients of the baptism of the Spirit, there was also a reciprocal attitude of appreciation for the clergy who were now expressing an active, supporting role in the search of vision the Lord was giving for a unified, ecumenical approach to healing. The vision is grand and beautiful and it has been captured in a few other communities we are aware of in the United States and Canada. It is a vision of a Christian hospital, staffed by Christians who are empowered with the gifts of the Spirit, dedicated to unity and support within the medical and religious fields and to basic ecumenism. The group is also committed to Christian follow-through, employing the various prayer communities in the state for the extended care of the Lord in love. "Special care" is not meant to imply that this hospital is to be exclusive or better or standing in judgment of other medical institutions but rather that it is a viable alternative, especially to the poor, but always supportive of the Lord's chosen healers wherever they are to be found.

Two realities emerged for us: (1) Although the group now grew steadily and doctors, psychiatrists, psychologists, nurses, pharmacists, substance-abuse counselors, social workers, dentistry technicians, etc., were involved along with persons who had spent years in the ministry of the various forms of Christian healing, we were only a drop in the bucket alongside the vision. (2) There was an urgency felt that the Lord intended us to move into some sort of public acknowledgment of what He was calling us to. We prayed and discussed, employing the composite wisdom of all in the group and when the first public announcement was made at Rhodes of what began in vision many months before—actually years for some of the people involved—it was made with the sense that the Christian Professionals would not lose their inspired hope until it was accomplished. In the meantime and starting that night, all of us together would have monthly healing services throughout the state and act as prayer teams with medical referral capabilities as well as employment of the Lord's gifts of healing. What interestingly developed was the sense that discernment, coupled with diagnosis, would eliminate a tremendous amount of confusion and unnecessary multiplicity which now surrounds medical referrals or Christian healing referrals that are given without such knowledge. A nurse equipped to discern causes, both medical and spiritual, of a particular patient's problem would be invaluable in making referrals. A patient treated first for a spiritually-caused cancer, for example, would then go to the medical doctor with no erratic symptoms.

In spite of this limited mode of operation there have been frustrations among us. The meetings have proceeded monthly as planned in various sections of the state. Concurrently, many members of the Christian Professionals meet monthly at St. Patrick's Friday evening prayer meeting to essentially minister in the same way. There may be, and often is, a referral made to counselors within the group but these sessions are limited to the time of the prayer meeting evening or healing service day. Each counselor and medical practitioner is still volunteering this time and cannot offer follow-up unless the person became a patient. As stated, one of the objectives in the vision presented to us was one place of healing where a patient might receive all the various forms of aid he needs with little or no confusion caused by referrals to first one specialist and then another. This applied as well to the Christian healing ministries and gifts. With this vision in mind it hurts us when we have to make referrals with limited follow-through capabilities of our own. Another painful realization shortly after we began was the need for many more people who are versed and experienced in both deliverance and inner healing ministries of the Spirit. Many more cases of this need among people were discerned than we originally thought would happen and after making some referrals we discovered that those in this ministry were overloaded. I believe many more of us are called to these ministries than those who say yes; perhaps all of us in our Christian walk in the Spirit are to be so equipped. Admittedly there is a need to be trained, a need for abundant wisdom and discernment as we move into these areas of healing—but far outweighing too much caution because of the dangers involved is the ever-present need evidenced every day in people who are deeply hurting in these areas and the many Christians like ourselves who also need the outpouring of this kind of love. More than ever before is the need for the saints of God to be equipped with power and authority and for the sons of God to arise—there can no longer be any question that indeed the world waits in travail for this to happen. One of the greatest criticisms that can realistically be spoken of the charismatic renewal concerns its overwhelming emphasis on authority, submission and community living. Improper balance of these areas can severely cripple the training and equipping of the saints to go out and do ministry. We've concentrated on the theology of Paul (and I love his theology as much as anyone) in building communities. This has left us unable, however, to carry out the great commission of Jesus to go into all the world baptizing in His name. We have grown in complication and forgotten some very simple things along the way. We should be able, in these days, to go out in the name of Jesus and bind Satan, touch any sick person in the street and command the spirits out of him or command him to get up and walk or call him to repentance and move on with the work of Jesus—to the next and the next and the next person who hurts and is sick.

Many times in our fellowship together the members within the Christian Professionals share their feelings of inadequacy and frailty but I praise God for their willingness, though weak they may be, to stand in a very bold place and offer the healing love the Lord so desires to give His people. They are all daring to go beyond their experience, out into the deep water of caring relationships. They affirm the Lord's promise that He will lift up His people.

Dr. Gendreau is now joined by Miss Jill Coleman and Sister Joan Glasheen in coordinating some forty medical and Christian healers in an ever-growing and far-reaching ministry toward the goal of total healing. Some of the members of the group have joined the

Association of Christian Therapists, headed by Father Francis MacNutt, an organization that is involved on a national level with the same vision.

Praise Gatherings

The sense of simplicity that has grown out of our relationships has taken on a more radical nature in our Wednesday Morning Group and has so become a part of our believing that we now involve ourselves in promoting and coordinating praise gatherings. We meet together at them, sending to our Lord the genuine rich and joyful praise He has given us and then we let Him do all the rest. For Rhodes we did give ourselves a name, "Rhode Island Christians for Renewal," and then on the program we listed our names and respective denominations. Now we don't even do that. We try to avoid the title "charismatics" when we meet but encourage the title "Christians." We no longer list our names and denominations. We are simply Christians, empowered by the Spirit, who love Jesus and want to share Him and be where He is.

The day we met to hear Dennis Splaine explain the vision he received five years ago in the streets of Seattle was an exciting and inspirational day for all of us. We had been growing in a sense of where the Lord was calling us to be active and, given the simplicity mentioned above, we were also beginning to pick up a sense of God's historic movement among us and especially in New England. Rev. Brad Campbell, recently of New England Tape Ministries from Chelmsford, Massachusetts, had shared with us already the vision the Lord had given him for New England which basically pictures the next, if not last, great world revival beginning in New England, particularly through praise and beginning particularly in Boston with the chains and bondages of Satan being broken through praise at the city gates similar to Joshua's battle plan at Jericho. The vision Dennis shared was that of building an increase in praise gatherings over the next several years that essentially would bring the people of God in New England to the point in God's plan of entering the Holy of Holies and approaching the very mercy seat of God cleansed, purified, sharing the bread and cup in oneness, offering continual incense by the Spirit of sweet-smelling praise. We were approaching a new holiness, a new righteousness, a new life of continual prayer for which we had been prepared over the beginning years of renewal. Dennis had already coordinated praise gatherings of huge magnitude the year before and as he shared his vision with us of our walking through the outer temple into the inner Holy of Holies, it struck a chord within that the Spirit had already implanted. Not long after Dennis shared with us in the early fall of 1977, the entire vision received the confirmation necessary in my own mind and heart, through Rev. Robert Whitaker of Glendale, California. Bob is the West Coast Coordinator for the Charismatic Renewal in Presbyterian Churches, a professor of history, and he is involved as representative to the movement of ecumenism especially in Los Angeles. The vision for New England was not foreign to him and fit well the prophetic sense that we do indeed stand upon the next, if not final, major wave of the outpouring of the Holy Spirit. That growth seemed to plateau in 1975 in the United States and provide a breathing spell for retrenching, solidifying, learning, honing of gifts, regrouping of forces to command sharper, more precise authority of faith. We stand, even now, upon the greatest spiritual explosion the world has ever known—it is new in God's history because, unlike any other revivals or renewal movements in history, this one is touching the whole world—every country, every denomination, every church, every street corner. The Spirit has been poured out on all flesh. Not a person is left untouched in some way by the Spirit of God in these days. The sense of adventure that Ladd Fields imparted to us way back in the beginning days of our walk in the Spirit was now taking hold as never before and I was thankful again for the gift of his life into ours. The apostle had gone before us all and truly prepared the way in our hearts for the coming of this day.

Our next gathering of praise then was to reflect the beginning of the Lord's claiming of His New England vineyard. National leaders were invited and two came to lead us in praise and teaching for a week. They traveled throughout Rhode Island and Massachusetts and coupled themselves in vision with another event culminating on the weekend of their departure in the Boston Park

Plaza, entitled the "Great Awakening '78" sponsored by other New England Christians in Massachusetts and Connecticut who share the same vision. Merlin Carothers and Charles Trombley poured out their lives for us and we've yet to discover the magnitude of the hundreds of miracles that took place in the deep praise that the people of God sent into His sanctuary.

In faith we believe Boston fell into the hands of the Lord's army. Soon to follow were Providence, Stamford, Hartford, Bridgeport, Portland—countless New England cities where the light of the Lord will outshine the darkness and the banner of His love will truly wave and be lifted high. There's little question in the minds of many that New England is the spiritual wasteland of America—a very likely spot indeed for the Lord to come in glory. This much He has shown us—that He moves and performs wonders beyond description in the praise of His people, especially and peculiarly where they have come together out of every Christian tradition, willing in their hearts to let go of their traditions long enough to love one another. And to this the people said, "Amen!" Out of the New England wastelands, on the final evening of a week of praise, 2,000 of us gathered at Marvel Gymnasium of Brown University and applauded our Jesus, the victorious Lord, who rode in amidst loud hosannas. Even the stones of Roger Williams' state of Rhode Island and Providence Plantations praised Him this night.

The Rhode Island State Council of Churches

Fellowship within the renewal oftentimes reaches very high levels of satisfaction and joy, for the renewal itself has been an open, noncondemning channel for people who want to share the deeper moments of their lives with one another. Tears of pain and joy are often shed as people reach out with abundant compassion and understanding to one another. A very gentle shepherding Jesus walks among His sheep as they pray and share. Often through sharing one another's love, Jesus looks into our eyes entreatingly offering to kneel before us to wash our feet with His own tears of joyful love and compassion for us. We learn to bless the Lord, to praise Him for the cross, to let Him wash us time and again. The open heart of love, the heart of flesh willing and ready to be kindled by the fire of Jesus' love, the outstretched hand of His love toward another gives so much life to us that we feel a truly unspeakable joy. This can also have a negative effect, however, of passing judgment upon less-fulfilling Christian relationships especially where Christian unity is involved. One of the usual targets of this negativism is the councils of churches who have over the years tried to bring about unity among Christians. Though their approach is usually quite different (church leadership downward to the people rather than the people upward) and the motivation sometimes different (because it is just and right and biblical as opposed to a response of the direct baptism of the Spirit), the theology and vision is much the same. Ironically, the approach toward unity within the councils of churches is generally much more accommodating than it is within the charismatic renewal and it is anathema to the more fundamental and pentecostal churches.

I would like to develop a few lines of thought within this section and offer some good-natured criticism that does not deal specifically with the Rhode Island State Council of Churches (RISCC) but which deals in the broader context of Christian unity and how it relates to the RISCC. Much of this relates to my own experience and how the Lord has dealt with me in the continuing story of His love for me, so certain basic premises are assumed:

1. The Lord loves His whole Church, visible and invisible. Although He may express His loving anger and wrath from time to time as opposed to His gentleness and sweetness toward various segments of His Church, He still is in the process of preparing His bride, unblemished and holy, to receive the Bridegroom. The churches of the book of the Revelation are seen as good in this or that regard but then the Lord speaks: "I have this against you," and it doesn't take too much imagination to see allegorically the churches of today fitting in the seven patterns.

2. We may codify the Lord's spiritual law toward holiness and righteousness so that it is helpful and clear but never, in these days, can we plumb the mysteries of God that are meant to be just that—mysteries!

3. In these days, where the Lord's children are in need of a

double portion of His grace, love and forgiveness they are receiving it; likewise, where they are in need of chastisement, they are receiving that. I never thought Hebrews 12 could be such a comfort but surely it is for those who are chastised to recognize it is happening because they are still sons.

4. Christian unity is not to come at all costs. (It will not happen at the expense of violation of the deep sensibilities of Christian people anywhere.) But likewise it is not to be stifled through traditionalism, judgment, envy, strife, pride and resentment.

With these premises in mind and the experiences out of which I come there are certain conclusions that make eminent sense to me.

1. The Holy Spirit is at work throughout Christendom and the world, leading people to Christ, and He is using every Christian organization, as well as non-Christian agencies, to accomplish His work. Some of this is clearly seen and demonstrable but some is still within the mysterious movement of our God and Father to be known in hope and faith. This does not exclude any grouping of Christians. There is obviously more power in some places than others because some groups of Christians are more open to receiving that power than others. But nonetheless, there are many gifts in the hands of the Spirit and He is capable of giving them where and how He will.

2. The councils of churches, mainline churches, non-denominational churches, pentecostal churches, charismatic churches, fundamental churches, evangelical churches, Christian ministries all the way from social justice to healing are all tools and instruments of the Holy Spirit today, some sharp and incisive, some dull and ineffective, some pocked and burred, some smooth and glittery, some tempered and hard, some soft and malleable, some being built, some worn out. When one of these can't be used it is pruned, thrown out or reground and retempered. When it can be used it is given more work and giftedness. And so the continual reworking of the Spirit toward the end that every knee shall bow and every tongue confess that Jesus Christ is Lord.

3. The greatest single detriment to unity is still man's greatest sin of pride which, though so often evident, rests below all others in the murky mystery of Adamic sin, plumbed only deeper by Jesus

Christ himself as He dwells in us. Only Jesus Christ then can be the center and totality of our unity! The Holy Spirit is being poured out on all flesh for the express purpose of the salvation of all men to implant Jesus Christ into the hearts of men and then to equip them with power and authority to lay claim to His kingdom. Jesus Christ will bring us into unity as He restores us and transforms us—as the master sculptor chips away at the stone of our pride inch by inch with His chisel of love down to the core of humility within us which is His. When we, along with Him, no longer count equality with God something to be grasped (Phil. 2 & 3), which is the root of our Adamic sin, when we, in all the authority and power of the Spirit at hand for us to use, allow for ourselves to be humbly vulnerable and silent even as Jesus, when we are truly hid in Christ, unity will be at hand and the world shall know Him who was sent by the Father (Ps. 8).

It is still our pride working deeply within us which allows us as councils of churches to accommodate nearly every group that comes along for the sake of unity. In this we sometimes clearly go against the Word of God. The Rhode Island State Council has granted affiliate membership to the Metropolitan Church of Providence, a self-confessing gay congregation espousing its homosexual orientation as one of the many acceptable life styles. They also espouse Christianity and Jesus Christ as their Lord and Savior. I believe they were voted membership because of the tremendous confusion about love that exists today. Christians, by and large, truly desire to be loving but often confuse what is loving with what is gentle and kind. Love indeed can be winsomely gentle and kind but it is never real love if it is devoid of truth and righteousness. I believe the Bible speaks clearly about the sin of homosexuality and says ultimately that Jesus and homosexuality cannot reside in the same person—sooner or later one must go. If we choose to let homosexuality go, then we must recognize it as against God's plan and treat it as we do any other sin. We must repent of it—willfully turn away from it. And this obviously cannot be done without great love and affirmation being given to the person involved. I have never witnessed anyone, myself included, who ever came to the Lord through judgment or fear, and maintain a healthy, growing relationship with Him. I've never noticed anyone who was caught in sin treated harshly and then return greater love. Paul clearly gives us a guide for treating those who are caught in sin in Galatians 6:1-5.

We treat them with the greatest gentleness, as if we were resetting a broken bone with no anesthesia. But if homosexuality is not seen as sin, the most unloving thing we can do is affirm the life style as if it were the person, speaking only a half-truth for the sake of love and unity. It won't and can't work that way.

This is all to say that the Holy Spirit of God was not withdrawn from the work of the state council of churches because of this. I believe it grieved and angered the Lord to be sure and I pray it will still provide the impetus for truth in this situation, but in the meantime, it has done something else. While the urban division of the council went on record against the endorsement of a similar self-espousing homosexual health service which counseled homosexuals of the rightness of their life style and drew little or no attention, the state council presidium drew fire from all quarters, many people withdrew their memberships and battle lines became clear. Inheriting the problem is the new executive director, Dr. Paul Gillespie, previously of Washington, D.C., where he pastored the largest integrated Baptist church in that city. Paul has tried to build bridges and I admire him greatly for both his evangelical stance as well as the gentle yet firm love of the Lord he demonstrates. I, like Paul, became equally disturbed over my brothers' quick judgment of the homosexual situation. The real problem is our deeper sin of pride.

It is equally our deep pride working within us that allows us as fundamentalists, evangelicals and pentecostals, and sometimes as charismatics to become so fear-ridden that we become judgmental and angry. I'm always cautious of people who claim they are speaking truth (as opposed to all around them) or who claim they are speaking a word on behalf of the Lord's anger. I don't doubt that this is possible but I'm usually more aware of the human fear and bitterness out of which a lot of these statements are made rather than the pure motivation of the Lord's love for the sinner. On many occasions, we found ourselves ministering to persons who had been casualties of this fearful judgment and although it indeed dealt with some particular sin they were involved with and found hard to shake off, I always found them repentant of the sin and willing to work in a positive direction when understanding and affirmation were given to them along with old-fashioned sharing. "Yes, indeed, I'm a sinner too. Let's pull out of this together." How cruel when Christians can so deeply hurt one another. The best way for us to correct one another's ways, if we feel seriously called of God to do so, is by our example of being at peace, cleansed ourselves of as much sin as possible and quick to admit the rest, in humility and with a great amount of the Lord's love and understanding surrounding us.

This rather prevalent judgment within the network of Christianity isn't reserved only for fundamentalists or pentecostals though they tend to be perhaps the most vocal. Indeed, the Lord has given these groups generally a good portion of the truth and they do know and love the Word. They have rich gifts to share with all the brethren but I know it will be squandered unless the means are the same as the end—the love of Jesus, firm to be sure but always humble.

A lot of criticism has flowed between the social activists and the more contemplative and studious Christians. They both eyeball each other in the subtle desire that the other would be "more fully Christian" like they are. It appeared for a while that the charismatic movement might bridge this particular gap and has, in some cases, found that Christians can have both a very deep prayer life and feed the hungry simultaneously. I believe the Lord has led us to do just that in Smith Hill but I'm beginning to realize there's something even greater beyond the charismatic movement. Though this movement of the Spirit is here to stay, it is meant to lead us elsewhere and my basic criticism of the charismatic movement is that it too easily falls into the trap of attempting to renew every tradition in its path. It soon succumbs to its own law and thereby loses the cutting edge of the Spirit. Mainline churches are viewed as dead and generally confused and desperately in need of opening up to the fullness of the Spirit. I couldn't agree more and know there is still ample cause to support the charismatic movement where it remains vibrant but some are called now, I believe, even beyond that—not to a new movement but to a very old one. Some are called to be Christians empowered with positive faith and authority—Christians modeled after first-century apostles, prophets and disciples. And these Christians, I'm pretty sure, will be found in the ranks of the charismatics, pentecostals, fundamentalists, nondenominationals, councils of churches, mainline churches, social activists, vicariates and Christian ministries. God loves the whole Church and is preparing the whole Church to be the bride of Christ. He has poured out His Spirit on the whole Church and has called His people to cease the envy and strife and fighting. I believe He has said simply and humbly, "I have called you all who bear the name of my Son. None of you has the whole and full truth. None of you has all the gifts of the body. None of you are the total body. Let there be some mystery in me that you don't need to know. Follow my leadings and know that you will all eat at the banquet table of life I have prepared. You will all live with one another throughout eternity so exhibit now the love I have given you for one another and, if you don't have enough love in you to gently reach out in unity to the brother who is in our family, then ask me for more and I will give it to you. Expect as sons of God to arise together, for I am still greater than all of you yet I am your loving Father."

I have been a member of the Urban Division now for the past eight years and have always found a sincere and dedicated commitment to Christ and His work through that division which tries to bring a unified Christian voice and resource into the peculiar problems of an urban society and fill a gap where denominations can't do the work alone. I've found the same joy in sharing and fellowship among the pastors in the division as I've found in the Wednesday Morning Group and although the style of prayer is quite different, I know they are all prayers from the heart and from His Spirit and they are heard by the same Lord Jesus and our Father. Paul Gillespie, executive of the RISCC and director of Urban Division, has done much to bring about a good feeling among evangelicals, charismatics, mainline Christians and social activists because of one factor—he unabashedly loves his Lord

Jesus, will say so anywhere he can and exhibits many varied gifts of that love. This is to say that he's not in love with the structure first and seldom if ever finds the need to criticize other Christian groups. He's too busy telling of the many facets of Jesus' love.

Atlantic City Conferences

Father Francis MacNutt, Mrs. Ruth Carter Stapleton, Father John Bertolucci, Robert Frost, Father John Randall, Father Michael Scanlan, Bob Mumford, David du Plessis, Father Jim Ferry and many others for the last four years, have led the Catholic Charismatic Christians of the Northeast in praise, teaching to 11,000 the first year, then 17,000, then 27,000 and last year 40,000. The world-famous boardwalk, now traversed by thousands on their way to gambling casinos, was for these four long holiday weekends in October during the last four years lighted up by the very face of Christ as hundreds of groups walked along singing praises to His name. Their hands were uplifted in prayer and they were always ready to touch someone for healing all hours of the day or night. These seemingly little witnesses were unnoticed by much of the world; but it should be noted that the entire boardwalk was covered with 40,000 people but policed by only one or two Atlantic City policemen. The convention hall was filled to capacity and the people sent up the explosive roar of Jesus to the very heavens and hushed to complete silence as the Spirit moved. There were many unsung stories of people praying with Atlantic City residents and families. There were weeks of preparation before each conference with Jim Ferry and members of his prayer community walking the streets of Atlantic City in claiming the city for Jesus Christ the Lord of all life. Other things that happened are now the subject of this section because of the magnitude of their importance in what the Lord has done.

For the last three years, Judy and I have been invited to attend the conference on the boardwalk as ecumenical guests and have joined approximately thirty to sixty pastors and their wives from the Protestant communities in the Northeast. Hundreds more were always invited but only we few ever found our way to what has become, I believe, the occasion for several bench mark experiences in the Lord's master plan of salvation and spiritual renewal throughout the world. As guests of the conference we were treated like royalty. Our hosts thoughtfully prepared the way for us to thoroughly enjoy the Lord with them.

In 1975, the conference leadership asked Father MacNutt, well-known author of several books on healing and a Jesuit priest (with one grandfather being Roman Catholic and his other grandfather being Presbyterian—an interesting aside for us), Mrs. Ruth Carter Stapleton, authoress of several books on inner healing and our president's sister, and Father John Bertolucci, pastor and charismatic vicariate head of the Archdiocese of Albany to lead the conference. St. Patrick's music ministry from Smith Hill was asked to lead in music, as they have each year, and we felt right at home. Through this leadership the Lord blessed us all with deep and rich miracles of healing and I believe three things happened of eternal significance.

1. Through Father MacNutt's gentle and holy teaching, conference participants were led to take the hand of Jesus and walk with Him as He led us into new relationships with our Father and we all experienced the joy of our Father in Jesus as He loved us in the special way of a brother. For many, this meeting was preceded by a sense of inner healing in our relationships with our own earthly fathers and then our Father in heaven as Jesus introduced us to Him as new brothers and sisters (also as new friends). We experienced our Father in a joyful, dancing, festive mood—a Father pleased and happy over us as we took our rightful places in the family of heaven, a Father deeply satisfied that we were now, more than ever before, open to His gentle, fatherly love. He was no longer to be the far-away, austere, harsh, uncaring Father that many of us had psychologically grown to accept; but He would now become the Father who would, at the drop of a hat, lift us up on His knee and hold us affectionately as we tearfully expressed our hurts and our joys. The "abba" that was Judy's first word in her prayer language was now fully understood and expanded for her and all of us to mean "Dad." We would cry, "Abba, Dad, Father. See me. Watch me. Hear my prayers. Thank you for loving me so much. Thank you, Dad, for my brother Jesus. I feel so close to you. Thank you."

Just to give one other example of the deep joy and happiness that prevailed throughout the conference, I recall in one of the early sessions when the Spirit led the 17,000 of us to sing gently in tongues and during the last strains of our singing, a soft clapping began and I remember thinking, "No, this is irreverent. Jesus, is it right?" He showed me a brief vision. He was walking down our row of people (as ecumenical guests we were seated in the front row, some eight feet from the stage), greeting all of us with an embrace. He had already passed me and was now greeting the people to my left. As I asked the question I saw Him turn back to me and there was a radiant smile on His face. Yes, indeed, it was all right. With tears then streaming down my face I couldn't clap hard enough. I think maybe others experienced the same vision because what started out as soft clapping ended in a deafening crescendo like the sound of thunder. Jesus, our gentle shepherd-brother, also our lion of Judah.

2. I believe the Lord used this occasion to pour out a unique and special gift of His love not just upon the conferees in Atlantic City but upon each and every family, church and prayer community out of which they came throughout the entire Northeast. There would be a new day of His love. A love powerful enough to again live out the pure and perfect standard of Jesus' life. A love able to turn our faces when slapped to be slapped again. A love deep enough to face the most bitter, rebellious onslaught this world has seen and yet stand. A love that would be able to transform the worst sinner into a lamb of God. A love that could no longer be satisfied with a half-truth. It was the fullness of the power of love that was to be appropriated in the months and years ahead, slowly but confidently and with new authority by all who confess Jesus toward the goal of sharing Him in a deep and real way whenever and wherever called upon to do so. And the gift is, I believe, still with us to this day—the Lord will not withdraw it because Jesus' victory is dependent upon the force of Jesus' love. It needs only to be recognized and used.

3. In the context of the power of this love, many resentments, divisions, and hurts were healed at the conference. Ruth Stapleton led in prayers of inner healing that ranged from very personal and

deeply painful separation among people to prayers that suggested healing of long-lasting institutional divisions. Prepared as we were by the Lord, we were all to go one step further. As Ruth Stapleton finished, Father John Bertolucci resumed with more prayers of healing for the churches. Protestants were asked to stand and Catholics who were next to them were asked to seek forgiveness from their Protestant brothers and sisters for all the pain and hurt caused by their church's offices over the past 400 years. We Protestants did the same. I shall always remember in my mind's eye what I saw at that moment. I looked up to the stage and saw Jake almost running across the forty-foot-long platform as determined as Peter was when he jumped out of the boat to be with Jesus on the shore. He came directly to Judy and me and we all cried. Through my tears I looked up again and saw Matt coming toward us, more slowly and gently but with tears already streaming down his bearded face. It struck me that in all the many hours we had shared together I had never known either Jake or Matt to shed tears. We stood together, embracing as one, weeping as one, stripped of our pride before the Lord. We were truly and deeply members of the same family and this night became, for all of us, the time when the Lord chose to heal 400 years of hurt, pain and division between the Catholic and Protestant churches. Even as I write this now the tears again fill my eyes both in remembrance of the great joy of healing gone by and the present pain that only two years after this night, in Kansas City, the Lord wept over His broken body. How we yearned with pure hearts in Atlantic City, 1975, to be one! And as children we played together in the fields of our Father's kingdom with Jesus our brother and with each other totally free of the thoughts of inter-church division and totally unaware and unsuspecting of the trials that lay ahead. On this night the Lord forgave the sins of our fathers. We were made into one family by the gift of the Spirit letting us freely give ourselves to our one Lord Jesus, who then showed us our one Father.

The next day the procession for the Mass was glorious. Three hundred priests entered to "The King of Glory" and the celebration became joyous. The cross bearer entered with an empty wooden cross—a resurrection cross—as if to say, "We love you, our Protestant brothers and sisters; we thank you for recognizing our obedience to the authority of our church in the Eucharistic celebration; we bear our cross as a sign to you of the love between us and as a symbol of what our Father has done for us all."

It was an exultant celebration for Catholic and Protestant alike and only joy and thanksgiving filled our hearts as we once again romped the fields together in our Father's kingdom.

By October, 1976, my spirit was beginning to be troubled and restless. Previous to the 1975 conference, I had been convicted that my love for people and especially those I was called to pastor was deficient and thus I prayed that the Lord would show me how to love more deeply. He had answered that prayer in Atlantic City by showing me the number of beautiful ways in which He loved me that I had never considered or received and I came home confident that He had filled me with a greater love. My preaching changed noticeably in that the Lord spoke through me a much greater hope and joy than ever before but there was no perceptible change in my relationships. In May of 1976 as I fulfilled my presbyter's responsibility of being a delegate to our General Assembly meeting in Baltimore, and facing there many issues before our denomination which anguished my heart, I prayed a very serious prayer asking the Lord to direct me about seeking another pastorate and about leaving Smith Hill. I also prayed about leaving the Presbyterian denomination which seemed to me then absolutely unresponsive to the Spirit and actively walking away from the Lord in so many issues she faced. The answers came back very clearly both in the sense of what seemed reasonable, prophetic, and from the Word. "No, not yet" as to leaving the denomination. And I felt a sense that the Lord still loved the Presbyterian church, would not forsake it, would continue to knock at her door and give her choices still of victory. As to my pastorate, "Give it one more try and if the people don't listen, shake off the dust from your feet and go." The greatest sense of call came, however, as He answered the prayer about Smith Hill. "No, stay, there is still much work to be done toward unity I have given." I had never separated my pastorate from the work on the Hill both in terms of our mission outreach in the early days as well as the Christian unity in later days and did not separate it in 1976. I believed they were to go hand in hand so I looked forward to a revitalization in the church as well as in our relationship with other churches.

We came to Atlantic City with the vision of the year before but with little having been accomplished in the year between in Smith Hill. We were to lead in a Communion service for Protestants on Sunday morning, as we had done the year before. I was to be a reactor, along with Ern Baxter and Bob Mumford of Christian Growth Ministries in Fort Lauderdale, to a talk prepared by John Bertolucci. At the ecumenical luncheon which happens each year for the ecumenical guests and the Northeast Catholic Charismatic Service Committee and speakers of the conference, John delivered a deep, heartfelt plea to his Protestant brothers and sisters for help in bridging the gap presented by the theologies of Mary, of authority, and of the Eucharist which so sorely divided us, because more basic than this, he protested, is our shared brotherhood in Jesus. I reacted mainly with the retelling of what I belive had happened the year before. Jake and Matt were both at the luncheon and were able to confirm the tremendous outpouring of love that had taken place and which still was able to both heap burning coals and cover a multitude of sins. The reconciliation of the churches since the Protestant Reformation and Catholic Counter-Reformation was mentioned. Concerning the theology of Mary, I spoke of an experience which had also happened the year before and which I would like to include here for its possible helpfulness. At the ecumenical luncheon of the year before I had related a story at the table about a discussion of Mary in our family that I thought was cute and humorous. After lunch, Judy mentioned to me that she thought what I said may have hurt one of the other persons at the table who didn't share my sense of humor about a very heartfelt topic. (Married Protestant ministers are gifted with wives who love them and supportively mention these things, thereby preventing future pain.) This began to work within me the conviction of the Spirit and during a workshop on "Purity of Heart" delivered by Joe Breault that afternoon I was led to pray for some help in this whole area of feeling about Mary. The room was filled with perhaps 250 people and was warm and close. No sooner had I prayed than a woman in the workshop began to make loud, gasping, screaming sounds. It was not a prayer in tongues but still somehow I sensed that the Lord was answering my prayer and much more quickly than I expected. The woman was taken out and someone in the assembly began praying the Hail Mary quietly. Everyone joined in and it was reverent and worshipful. The Lord spoke clearly to my heart that Mary was indeed a very special human being chosen out of all others to be the handmaiden of the Lord. She was indeed to be reverenced. I thought immediately of the special feelings I have had for Peter and Paul and John and Thomas of the New Testament and of the warm feelings I had and continue to have for all the saints of God today and it struck me that I had avoided Mary simply because it was in my tradition to do so, but now the Holy Spirit has set me free to see her as presented in the Word and with all the fullness that may mean. The Holy Spirit has also done the same with Catholic priests I know who say, as I would, that it is important always to recognize Mary's primary role of pointing people toward Jesus and leading people to Him just as did Peter, James, John, Paul, and just as the Holy Spirit does. She, like the apostles, does not ask to be worshiped. Rather, they ask that we see Jesus through them. If we pictured a church with Jesus preaching from the pulpit and saw Mary right in the front row being the first among all to praise Him, we would also see her directing all others by the purity of her example toward an open, free, devoted and self-sacrificing worship. She has much to show us about life in the Spirit and from the view of humanity there was no other person who knew Jesus like she did.

There are many good bridges that can be built in our understanding of Mary. Protestants need to open up to new understandings which the Lord will faithfully show us. Catholics, on the other hand, need to recognize that Protestants, who base their understanding upon the Word, and who must look more deeply at what it means for Mary to be the mother of Jesus cannot by this then look at her as the mother of God and deify her. I do not agree with some Catholics who believe that Mary will be the one to unify the Christian Church. Jesus Christ alone can do that. We can, however, all grow in reverence for Jesus Christ as we try to emulate Mary.

After sharing this experience from the previous year's conference, I sat down and, shortly after, we adjourned to our next meetings. It was not until the conference of 1977 that the Lord provided some possible answers concerning the Eucharist which I'd like to treat separately in another section.

Not much was mentioned about Christian unity outside of the ecumenical gatherings specifically planned for the 1976 conference. During Sunday's Mass, Jake gave the homily and I remember great pride welling up within me that it was my special brother who was sharing in the Lord's glory this day. He spoke ironically enough about Mary. Moments before, the cross bearer had led the procession again of more than 300 priests but the corpus of Christ again hung upon the cross.

It was chilly in Atlantic City, during the conference of October, 1977. Judy was unable to go with me this year and my own participation changed also. I had been asked earlier in the year to speak in a workshop entitled "Charism and Ecumenism" and as the time drew near, the panel I would be with was determined. Father John Bertolucci would lead, David du Plessis, Father Richard McAllear and I would speak. David du Plessis was also one of the major speakers of the convention. Though not much had happened in the relationship between our church and St. Patrick's over the year there were specific instances of deep sharing, some of which are mentioned in the next section concerning the Eucharist. The Wednesday Morning Group was on the heels of Rhodes and already we were beginning to share with Dennis Splaine concerning the next praise gatherings in 1978. Some of the men in the group then attended the Kansas City conference and returned to us with a report of what had happened. They shared with us the pain and suffering of the Lord over the division of His body. Though now some of the pain we were experiencing was validated, it didn't ease the sense of hurt that brothers once melded together in love were growing apart and, though we knew the love was still there, now there were some new resentments too. As the conference approached, I found myself growing in a bolder healing ministry and at the same time, yearning for the completion of our participation in the vision being presented for the praise gatherings in New England, of entering the Holy of Holies of our Lord God. But these had to do with both personal gifts and yearnings; their application seemed most active in the United Presbyterian Church and the larger Christian community of Rhode Island and, not to say this was wrong or bad, it had little to do with the deep commitment we had made years before to renewal of our churches and the unity which would develop from natural renewal and close proximity.

What was happening in Smith Hill, the place where God chose to touch down and set a city upon a hill? Here, unlike any place in the Northeast that I had yet heard of, there was a chance for exemplary unity. I was growing more and more frustrated and bitter at the new rigidity of our churches and what seemed clear evidence of new legalisms which were preventing the clear flow of the living Spirit. What was getting in the way? Why the dark cloud? I was quick to judge—and laid most of the blame at the feet of my Catholic brothers who no longer seemed interested in unity at all. We had given so much. They had given so much, but now internal problems were taking total precedence over our shared life together and the vision was slipping away. The days were growing longer and darkness was coming. We deceived ourselves into thinking we were still walking in the light. What could I say in the workshop? I was also asked to speak at the ecumenical supper. What could I say at the supper? My soul began to experience anguish, the beginning of several months which would carry me once again into the deepest pit of hell. The time for the conference came and while driving down with Ken and Claudia Steigler and Andy LePenta, I shared my anguish. They too felt the same pain and emptiness. I knew Judy also felt the impending seriousness of these days. I don't recall now the first evening's general session but upon arriving and looking over the programs of the two tracks and workshops provided, there was no recognition of unity beyond what always appeared and more to my dismay only an optional film being shown from Kansas City with no other mention. The only ecumenical function was our workshop. I stayed up all night praying and working on the workshop for the next day. I worked all the next day until 3:00 when the workshop was to take place. I was listening to tapes of previous praise gatherings, listening to a tape of Jake's teaching the year before at a large ecumenical gathering in Attleboro, Massachusetts, listening to a wedding Jake and I performed together during the summer—yearning for hope, for love, for understanding which had been so very much a part of our shared lives together. Why now, for the first time in my life, was I being so overwhelmed by feelings of abandonment, anger and pain?

Now in the same hall where the Lord had allowed me to see His beaming, radiant, smiling face as we clapped our praises of joy three years before, He allowed me to see another vision. This time I wept tears of bitterness, hurt, anger and pain. I saw my son struck by an automobile and his body broken. I lashed out momentarily in anger and frustration and pointed an accusing finger at the Eucharistic table and said, "It's because they will not allow me to come to the table!"

"No, Tom," the Lord said gently, "it's because of you." My tears softened to grief and remorse. It's only now that I more fully understand that vision for myself but I understood some of it then to be a partial, yet infinitely small, sharing of our Father's pain at the broken body of His Son and this I shared, with the positive experiences of the past year, in the workshop. The Lord used it all, the four of us, and the gentle hearts of 2,000 people who crowded in the room and overflowed out of the doors to find us all weeping and mourning with Him over the broken body of His Son, even as He called us to do in Kansas City. We had touched a little bit of His holiness. I had reached a summit after a long, five-year climb. There was a long, straight fall ahead which I did not see. Though it had begun in the vision of my son with my anger, I was to keep one foot on the summit awhile longer, believing the unity we knew as children romping the fields of the kingdom was being restored.

A Shared Suffering

The cup of blessing which we bless, is it not a participation in the blood of Christ? The bread which we break, is it not a participation in the body of Christ? Because there is one bread, we who are many are one body, for we all partake of the one bread. (1 Cor. 10:16-17)

I would like to preface this section with a few words concerning the perspective from which I speak. I believe there are very few absolutes with the Lord and they are all quite manageable. Our tendency, however, is to complicate and legalize our spiritual life and the spiritual growth of others which, in time, becomes stifling and unmanageable. There is purpose to the law. "For freedom Christ has set us free; stand fast therefore, and do not submit again to a yoke of slavery" (Gal. 5:1).

The charismatic renewal has greatly simplified Christian faith and done away with numerous bondages to the law. Most of us in the renewal have grown to expect this and deeply welcome these directions of freedom and simplicity. This also intensifies our pain when the renewal itself gets more complicated or submits to new law. It's not coincidental that so many have been brought into renewal in Jesus through someone, by the Spirit, who loves them from another Christian denomination, social background, etc., for through that experience of love, the Lord breaks down barriers of law that have existed for centuries. In the twinkling of an eye. Peter and Cornelius, through a gift of the Holy Spirit (a vision), opened their lives to Jesus, loved each other and church history was changed. Now the gospel would go in fullness and not half-truths, not in Phariseeism or spiritual superiority to the Gentiles. God's plan to spread His salvation to the entire Gentile world employed a charismatic gift, openness to Jesus, willingness to give up law and tradition, the Spirit's love and two men of completely different backgrounds and orientations. Indeed, they could easily have been enemies. It was a simple, glory-filled event. Then we set in for centuries of complications and laws until the time God set for the outpouring of His Holy Spirit on all flesh—until today when the simple act of love in Jesus by the power of the Spirit once again supersedes all law and boundaries. I believe the twentieth century is the most exciting century in which to live since the first century, because God is moving, as He did then, to bring about a new time altogether unknown to the experience of man. It seems we are sitting on the threshold of His glory. Never before has the potential for the unity of the body of Christ been so before us. Again the time has fully come. The prophecy of Joel is being fulfilled before our very eyes. The prayer of Jesus in John 17 is being answered by the Father before our very eyes. Indeed, we are the answers to these prophecies and prayers. God has chosen our instrumentality to bring about the next, if not last, cataclysm of history. We embark on a new age, and proclaim a kingdom at hand in a way our ancestors never could. They hoped. We see. Hallelujah!

But a word needs to be shared at least for this particular time, perhaps for the present decade. I see out of my own pain and spiritual journey an anguished tragedy that we are doing little to avoid. *This new age must be entered in unity.* This I believe is God's word and not mine though my Spirit responds from the depth of my soul to that word. We have learned that unity must be real, grounded in Jesus' love and with Him as our head. It needs to be real and start from the bottom among the people—not from the top among the theologians or dreamers or authorities (though the Lord prepares hearts through them too). That lesson has been good. Our caution and desire not to walk ahead of Him has been wise. But we have made a new law out of our caution. We have become complacent as He pointed out to us at Kansas City, 1977. He weeps. Our caution, legalisms and complacency now cause pain to God. We need to repent in the sense of being determined to change. I would like to share my experience in this regard.

The Mass was beautiful. The gifts of the Spirit and love for Jesus brought tears to my eyes. As we approached the time of the Eucharist I was feeling a great sense of expectancy. A few of my close and loving Roman Catholic brothers and sisters told me, with tears in their eyes, that they would pray a special infilling and anointing for me at that time. I felt their prayers and somehow knew in my spirit I had received the body and blood of Christ though I did not go to the table. We receive Jesus in so many ways: in prayer, in the Word, through love, in the Eucharist. How? For what purpose? To what degree? All His to give and so shrouded in the mystery of who He is and His love for us. In truth, it's sufficient for us to be open and to know we have received Him. We truly need to make no laws concerning this. I, for one, am willing to wash clean the theological battleground of how we receive Jesus in the Eucharist and simply confess, "I receive the body and blood of Christ as He intends me to; I receive Jesus; I am in His presence; it is a mystery I need not fathom."

As I attended Mass on one occasion or another as an expression of our love for one another and the unity the Spirit has brought about, I began to lose the sense of infilling and anointing that I first experienced through the love of my brothers and sisters. Though I could rejoice with them and for them, I began to experience more and more pain. My joy left as we would approach the Eucharist and my heart would begin to weep. I found myself needing to pray constantly and earnestly just to keep a smile on my face and allow my brothers and sisters to continue to feel their love for me. I didn't enjoy this pain and stopped going to any Masses whenever I could do it gracefully, though all through the week we would share His love in a thousand other ways. As mentioned before, it's not uncommon for us in our neighborhood to find little groups of Christians praying together or praying with someone with a need. No one is concerned if the group consists of all Catholics, Protestants or non-church people. We all love Jesus and that's enough. We share meals, money, concerns, pain, mission. We pass out cups of cold water continually together. We find ourselves doing all of Matthew 25 together. Many of us have discovered this new glory of God operating (John 17) as we minister and share our lives together. When we are in prayer meetings together there is a glory of God present that is not in any of our individual prayer meetings. More healings take place and more visions and understandings emerge concerning Jesus' work and the Father's plan to one day unite all things.

We live and share all life together. Our sons and daughters marry each other. We confess our sin together. But when the Lord invites us to His table, only requiring that we love Him and have recognized our need for Him and only saying that we must have reconciled with our brother—when He simply says that we who are heavy-laden and burdened may come and find rest in Him and we can't go to the Communion table because the church says we cannot—the pain becomes nearly unbearable. It is perhaps even more difficult because the Presbyterian church (though admittedly as a church equally and seriously sinful and just as bound by law as any other church) excludes no one from the table of the Lord and I've always known that open invitation. I have always rejoiced that our church didn't try in this way to come between the believer and his Lord.

A series of events this last year began to offer new hope for effectively dealing with our spirituality and humanity co-existing in this regard. It began in my own family. Two of our children attend St. Patrick's Grammar School, a charismatic ministry of St. Patrick's Parish. It's a beautiful school. Teachers, parents, and administrators are all looking to Jesus as they share love with each other and the children. They are sensitive to the Spirit leading the children, and deeply aware that the children are tomorrow's prophets, healers, preachers, deep lovers of Jesus. In many real ways they lay down their lives that the children will not only learn the three R's but, more importantly, know His love.

My son was in first grade and had, with his class, learned about the Eucharist in preparation for their First Communion. When these kinds of things happen, we try to consider ways to lessen the pain, certainly not highlight it, and it became a special burden since it was seven-year-olds who were growing so naturally in His love and teaching us so much. Judy and Ken's teacher, Miss Michele Berg, first discussed what might be done. They both wept as the thought came from their hearts across their minds that I might, through the pastor's and bishop's permissions, give Ken Communion under the offices of the Presbyterian church while Father Kelly, pastor, would serve the host to all Ken's classmates. It was only four years ago that the United Presbyterian Church allowed for young children to receive Communion prior to Confirmation. Liturgically it could be accomplished with little effort. The thought was shared with the principal of the school, Sister Mary Mahoney, and this brought more tears as it did when Judy quietly shared the thought with me. I was to see Father Kelly. By the time we actually talked, other thoughts had crossed my mind and, trying to avoid a confrontation, (which has always been my nature) they took precedence over the original thought which I believe the Spirit truly inspired yet which probably would have ended in more pain for all of us. I have grown to realize that we are all victims of this. We must continue to love one another with the Lord's sensitivity in spite of all the pain. This experience is a precious gift from the Lord and one which we do well to seek.

Anyway, the thought which finally took shape, which we accepted and planned for, was for Ken to be an intercessor for his classmates from a very special and prominent place up front with his family, principals and teachers while his first-grade friends each came forward to receive the host. Maureen Reynolds, another first grader and Roman Catholic, had decided to wait to receive her First Communion and all were comforted by her honesty and individuality, the church's flexibility to protect her freedom to decide, and that Ken would not be alone. (Maureen has since received her First Communion and it was a profound joy for us all.) And to honor Ken, the first-grade children, their parents, teachers, principals and friends would attend our church the next time we were to observe Communion so they could share their love with Ken while he partook of the elements. Though we did not know it then, this was to pierce the hearts of many of my brothers and sisters who were attending a Protestant Communion for the first time and, while we offered an open table, they chose to decline. For the first time we were now to share the fullness of this pain together.

But this was just the beginning. In between these exchanges of the first-grade class, Judy and I attended a Black Heritage Lunch at our branch library that had been coordinated by Mrs. Mary Jones, one of the librarians who was also one of the elders of our church. She had asked her class to research various important black personalities in the history of Rhode Island and to share their findings with those attending the luncheon. One personality was presented who did not come from Rhode Island but who has had a profound effect on the unity of all people—Rev. Dr. Martin Luther King. We heard again those oft-repeated words from the steps of the Lincoln Memorial:

I have a dream that one day on the red hills of Georgia the sons of former slaves and the sons of former slaveowners will be able to sit down together at the table of brotherhood.
(From "I Have a Dream" by Martin Luther King, Jr., August 28, 1963)

I have a dream that one day we will sit down at the Lord's table together. All our eyes filled as Mary's young daughter Angela read the speech and my heart pained although I did not fully appreciate why. I thought it was the pain I also feel that we still are so far away from the true love of whites and blacks for each other. So much blood has been shed and yet we still harbor such fear and hate for one another. But I was to discover again that there was more.

One of the dynamic young couples of our community was to be married in late summer. We have all shared deeply in their joy. They met for the first time in the presence of many of us who were attending our ecumenical Easter sunrise service in front of the Capitol Hill Interaction Council's building where much of our reaching out together to the poor takes place. We watched their love begin and, like a flower, it has been an object of beauty to behold as it unfolds in various formations and takes on richer shades of color. Bob is an elder in our church and Margo is a member of St. Patrick's, a part of the Word of God Community and originally a member of their music ministry. They had asked Jake and me to perform the ceremony. Jake and I were honored and thrilled to work together as we always are. Again, however, we were faced with the Eucharist. The congregation would be a mixture of different denominations. Bob is Armenian and his family still attends the Eastern Orthodox Armenian Apostolic Church in our neighborhood. Since Bob is an elder in our Presbyterian church, there would be Eastern Orthodox, Protestant, and Roman Catholic people in large proportions. And since Bob was executive director of the Capitol Hill Interaction Council and in contact with people of all traditions, there would also be many people of nonchurch backgrounds there. Bob and

Margo were committed to their wedding being a witness of unity. They are both deeply in love with the Lord and felt that the sacrament of their marriage was to be shared in this special way. But how should they handle the sacrament of the Eucharist?

The wedding was to be in St. Patrick's sanctuary. Bob and Margo decided to approach the Bishop of Providence, Louis Gelineau, with the request that I be allowed to concelebrate the Eucharist (in the fashion suggested for my son's First Communion). The bishop, sensing most deeply their desire to present unity, suggested they not observe the Eucharist as it could dramatize disunity instead. He encouraged them to highlight in every way possible the unity they desired only through the sacrament of marriage. He could not at this time allow me to concelebrate. Bob and Margo prayed about this several times and continued to hear the Lord indicate His desire for them to have the Eucharist.

We examined all sorts of alternatives. I was careful not to show all my pain because a wedding is not the place for such feelings to be worked out. Too many weddings are robbed of all the joy that should surround the bride and groom, by families, past mistakes, or other circumstances and even though Bob and Margo deeply felt this sense of mission toward unity, I did not want to impair their joy. Some of the suggestions, therefore, indicated a sense of levity; maybe I could pass out flowers to the Protestants and Orthodox as the Catholics received the host, or maybe we could have Bob and Margo ride in a horse-drawn carriage with the congregation following from St. Patrick's to the United Presbyterian Church with each church serving its own Communion. But we knew we were unrealistically skirting the issue. We did not want to submit to half-truths any longer. At the final meeting we had concerning this, Jake made a suggestion out of his experience which lifted our hearts immediately because of its honest and truthful approach. He suggested we have the Eucharist, but ask Catholics not to receive it in recognition of the pain in the broken body of Christ, to share in mourning with the Father over the broken body of His Son still existent, and to share a realistic love with their Protestant and Orthodox brothers. He would celebrate, I would stand beside him, he would receive and give to the bride for the whole congregation. Now I realized the full impact of my pierced heart at the Black Heritage Luncheon. When blacks could not go into a white southern restaurant, their white brothers would not go in either until they could go to the table together. And so they would meld their lives together and share the suffering of separation until unity was allowed. Suffering is the cement of love. The building of our love here in Smith Hill was to receive some much-needed mortar cement because bricks were beginning to fall out.

Bob and Margo's wedding was beautiful. Some Japanese Shintoists and French atheists who were guests of one of the attendant families came that day and were touched with Jesus' love during the wedding—a simple and profound fruit. They went forward to receive the host the next day. I was touched deep in my heart with a renewed love. Now I knew, as never before, that when my Catholic brother said he loved me, he truly meant what he said. He was willing to give up at least that one day the most meaningful sacrament of his life to show me his love and no longer accept this precious, God-given source of life as a tool of separation. To our knowledge this moratorium has not been declared before though it is ecclesiastically proper, however irregular and undesirable it may also be in light of our desire for full participation.

It became our hope that the same moratorium might be declared at the upcoming Eastern Regional Catholic Charismatic Conference in Atlantic City, 1977, for the Saturday observance of the Mass for the same reasons. If Bob and Margo's wedding was indeed as prophetic as we felt it was and if the prophetic word of our Father concerning His pain over the broken body, calling us to mourn and weep, had filtered down with any of this kind of understanding, then perhaps this could become a clarion call, a ground swell that church authorities and theologians might recognize as a seriousness about unity not yet heard. This was our hope. The conference leadership, after hearing a heartrending plea from Matt Tierney on our behalf and struggling in prayer and pain for one whole day, decided it was premature; however, they agreed that it was right. A challenge was and is issued to consider this as an interim voluntary step which is real and expressive of the present life the Lord is sharing with us toward the end that one day we will sit at His table together. This is the hope of the ages, the desire of our Father, the prayer of our brother, and the pain of our hearts.

St. Augustine suggested, "Love God and do as you please." It sounds like something a saint would say. The road with Jesus *is* a road of growing sainthood. However, while our humanity still needs law, our sainthood needs freedom. To be hid in Christ is to be totally free. If the charismatic renewal begins to set new laws or embellish old laws it becomes a half-truth and we must look beyond it. The Lord has promised the outpouring of the Spirit upon all flesh. The visible church today is only one small part of that, the church's traditions a yet-smaller part. In such tension and potential confusion, it's important to recognize the need for order (law) but only as a means to freedom. If we hang on to what was right last year we may well miss the cloud moving this year into a new dimension. It's a particular inherent danger in parish renewal as we become entrenched with the commitment to renew everything the parish is or was. It's a particular inherent danger in denominational renewal as we seek to renew every agency, every vicariate, every church, every judicatory in the denomination.

I believe we must be determined to repent, to turn around, and be the family our Father now calls us to be. We must enter this new age in unity. I'm convinced it is one of the most profound reasons why we are being renewed as we are by the Spirit in these days. It is Jesus who is lifted up when we're together and He is One.

Tradition tells us of John, the disciple who laid his head on Jesus' breast, the one whom Jesus loved in a special way and when he was very old he would be carried into churches to share the Lord Jesus with them. He would say only, "Love one another as He loved you." He would repeat this over and over again until they tired of hearing him. Love one another as He loved you—a good absolute to take into our hearts. What unity there would be if we would practice this.

Rochester and David du Plessis

We were on the road long before the sun came up and Phil Sheridan was sharing with Judy and me some of the fruits of the positive faith message he had been teaching various church groups in Rhode Island. The plane leaving Logan International Airport to get us to our Rochester appointment by 9:00 A.M. would carry eleven of us from Rhode Island for a day of meetings with David du Plessis. Ken Steigler had arranged for the trip and his long-time personal friend, Don Reiling of Christian Center, in Brockport, New York, would host our stay. In a sort of reflective way, it was another chance for me to rediscover my roots. We would also spend a day with my dad before returning to Providence. I was reminded of October, 1976, just before the Atlantic City conference. On that occasion we had gone back for an anniversary celebration at the church I had grown up in as a youngster, became a member of, and from which I received my first instructions and fellowship in the Christian faith. At that time, I had very vivid impressions; first, the memories rushed in of the countless hundreds of times our family and I were in that building for worship, suppers, programs, youth fellowship, Sunday school—it was the center of much of our life. They were good memories of a loving people and a wholesome surrounding. The night we all gathered for the anniversary celebration brought many of the same people back together again. Some, of course, were not there. My mother never recovered from open-heart surgery in 1969 and some of her best church friends were also gone. My brother who was sent from the church as a junior-year-abroad missionary in 1953 to the Philippines was in California fulfilling his duties as a grammar school principal. Dad and I went together but since I was at the head table we did not sit together, unlike the many, many times of my childhood when we sat at the same table as a family.

Judy was home taking care of our children. Although she was not a part of most of the memories I held in my heart of a secure childhood in this church, she and I are one and I missed her too. The whole evening and next morning's worship service brought to mind again a certain kind of loneliness and sadness that I've become accustomed to but nevertheless it still exists. The church had, by and large, not changed much from the way I remembered it because so many of the same people were still there. Not many of the young friends I had grown up with were there, but it was their parents and aunts and uncles who had remained faithful or who had not moved away or were interested in an evening of remembrances like this, but who had also befriended us all as children and held a special place in my heart. I was the first one to leave the church for the ministry and they all felt a sense of pride in one of theirs who had been called. Indeed, I had been called and set apart, never again to sit at the table or in the same pew with my family to worship. The life of a minister or priest or counselor or healer or apostle and his family is called to be a dynamic one which is able to embrace the whole family of God and find roots in the enigmatic Spirit of God rather than in returning to the secure and loving relationships of the past. It is a life that can only grow when it finds its basic fellowship with God and then proceeds to fellowship with people. Friendships once based on affinities and shared experiences with those close to us become guarded relationships of pastoral care for the whole flock of God entrusted to your keep. Though in shepherding there are deep and rewarding relationships and the genuine comfort of the Spirit as we walk in empathy with one another through life's deepest hurts and joys, there is a reality that we can never become friends. Care for the whole flock means special nurturing for each one and at least part of this caring says that, though all are special to God and at times need very individualized love, none is to become greater than another as the object of your attention or heart feelings.

So these two things are at work in the pastorate: (1) because of the calling, there is constant growth in the Spirit, constant change, constant dying to holding on to anything that offers worldly security; and (2) again because of the calling, a need to develop an overall approach to people from the Lord's point of view of total giving to each yet never one over and above the other. To be sure, the Lord blesses this richly. I've never known such joy as when I've been used of God to bring another into a relationship with Jesus Christ as Savior and Lord and thus into the eternal family of God. It's indescribable. And I always rejoice when I see the people of God trying even harder to love each other because the pastor has not caused jealousies or envy to exist by his own culling out of special friends. In chapter eight I mentioned the need for friends and here I express the dangers of this. The balance comes in the recognition of our humanity and being careful in the Spirit not to hurt or offend a brother. If we genuinely love all, we can be blessed by a variety of relationships without deeply hurting any.

I could reminisce, cry and laugh just like all the rest did that evening. But I could not share much more, for they would stay in their church home and I would go on to a church home much more enigmatic. I also reflected on something else. My spirit also grieved that evening because, in spite of the fact that it was an evening of remembrances, I heard too much and too often the pleading of the human heart to return to the good old days. Oh! How deeply I could understand yet how much more deeply I know that it can never happen nor should we ever seriously entertain the notion it should. To be sure, there was goodness then—it was the Lord's church then too—and we're asked to remember, to rejoice and praise and thank Him for His mighty works but conversely we're never called to repeat the same situation again. And the evidence of too much of this feeling of hanging on was there, for the hall that night was not packed with young people, either in age or in the Lord, regardless of the program. I've not known a church yet that has not been resistant to change nor where generations of the same family have not filled her seats. As golden as this may be, and there can be deep rewards from long-term commitments and fellowships among people, lest we open ourselves to the moving of the Spirit which is a wind that blows where it will and cannot be restrained or tied down, our churches will die, not to mention the fact that we will be very ill-prepared for the days that lie ahead. As much as I may yearn for the past and let my heart turn over for those days of security and innocence, if I do so I know I will die in the Spirit. I must not, and I now cannot, not only because of my calling as a Christian minister, but even more basic than that, because of my calling as a Christian—the same calling that any of you reading this book shares with me. I know I must let go of the golden dreams of the past, I must put to death the feelings of the heart that try always to lock things in place and offer a seeming security at the time. I must, as you must, continue to push out on the choppy water and learn to walk on top of it. Peter, James and John on the transfiguration mountain experienced an indescribable spiritual joy and infilling. Their very first thought right straight out of their hearts and guts was to hang on to it—and they gave a very good argument for doing so. Jesus' very first thought, however, out of His wisdom and love was—"No, let it go, don't build a booth in remembrance. Choose life—not death." We must grow to learn simply that the future is in our Lord's hands; ultimately it has to be good because it comes from His deep, mysterious love for us all. We don't have to understand it all; we merely need to pluck up our faith, strengthen our weak knees, lift up our drooping hands, and walk into the wind of His dynamic Spirit. If you're tempted to walk backwards, away from the wind, to the secure, peaceful cove of the past—as you most surely will be tempted to do—don't go.

I knew as the plane sped on its way to Rochester this time, I was not going in reverse but forward in my spiritual walk. We were going to spend time with David du Plessis which had to be only a time of forward movement. And our time with dad was to be a time of beautiful sharing and support. The week previous to our Rochester journey I announced my resignation to the elders of my pastorate at United Presbyterian. Almost ten years of ministry in the church, for me, meant that I had retreated to the peaceful cove. The Lord was speaking to me in Baltimore two years previously and I did try to watch closely for the signs. We did grow in the church; I was encouraged. But the Lord was also speaking of other things and then made it clear to me that now was the time both for me and the church to seek deeply and actively the next step of His will for us.

I listened hard to David as he spoke. He said many of the things he had discussed in Atlantic City in our panel workshop almost six months before and they again touched the spirit deep within me. He spoke of things I had believed before I heard him share and of movements we had already experienced in Rhode Island. But he told the thirty or so of us gathered that day something else I did not remember from Atlantic City or from the book *A Man Called Mr. Pentecost* which Bob Slosser wrote with him. I was so intent upon what he was saying because I knew the Lord would speak a word to me through him about the choppy waters we were now treading.

The word did come. It's the only one I can specifically remember now and it came directly from David's life experience. It did not tie together then but the Lord knew and spoke it in such a way that I, and probably everyone else there too, would not forget it. It went deep into my spirit to be pondered and only much later did it connect with Baltimore, with the vision of my son's broken body I received in Atlantic City, with the prophecies of Kansas City and, more poignantly, with my personality. I've discovered that we can be insensitive to the early promptings of the Spirit's desire to move on in us or be deceived in His leadings to correct our course, and all in the Lord's name and for His sake we can direct our own ship into troubled waters. There's an element of blind faith and courage involved in course corrections again that we must, but are not always willing to, put forth.

David paused after speaking of some of the pain of rejection he has felt so many times in his life when people and churches could not hear the message the Lord had placed upon his heart to give about unity. "But," he said (and I'm paraphrasing), "I remember the Lord as He wept over Jerusalem and I remember the Lord as He overturned the tables in His Father's house and whipped the moneychangers. Jesus is the Judge, not David, and in all these years I've never whipped. I've only wept." And then he had to sit down, for the Lord had again given him tears before us and he sobbed quietly as we began to pray.

Snow still lay deep upon the ground from the blizzard of '78 as Judy and I said good-by to dad and boarded the plane for Providence. The Lord had taken me back to roots so deep that I would only discover them much later as I learned for the first real time in my life to rest in His Spirit.

This is what I learned. I had allowed the pain of separation between my Catholic brother and myself to build up unconfessed resentments within me. I chose to passively deal with this in forgiveness but was to discover that the forgiveness I confessed inwardly needed to be actualized through my own repentance and it needed to be shared with my brothers. I was loving with a half-truth. In repentance and humility we can paradoxically move toward speaking and sharing love with ever-greater authority and victory. Because I didn't do this, my hidden resentment was sufficient cause for brokenness in the body. As I began to learn this and did move in my spirit toward repentance, I found I could also rest in His Spirit in a new way because I knew again He still loved me in my spiritual failure and need for spiritual rest.

The eleven of us who went from Providence out of the Wednesday Morning Group had taken one more step together in bonding our love. We were still planning the week of praise with Merlin Carothers and Charles Trombley. We decided then to invite David to come to Providence (he has often been in our city—even as many as thirty years ago—meeting with pentecostals at Zion Bible Institute). It will be to my knowledge, however, the first time he will come to Providence to share with main-line Catholic and Protestant Christians as well as classical and neo-classical pentecostals and charismatics. It was planned for November, two months following the world-wide gathering of Christians at Singapore and one month following the first Catholic Charismatic Conference for New England in Providence. We were inspired with new hopes and visions and were ready to pursue a very old-fashioned idea with a new flair—tent meetings.

Hopes and Visions and Tents

Our tent was the open sky and our sawdust the broken bottles on the streets and sidewalks and beer cans in the parks as we preached, sang, and praised God to any who would come. There were times at each tent meeting for persons to receive the Lord or to come for prayers of healing. The Christian Professionals also participated. The Lord knew who would come and it would be the very humble people of the world, the outcasts, the obvious sinners. And we witnessed His glory, especially in music, a glory that lifted us into the heavens. What He allowed us to see actualized is not far from the hope He originally gave us through vision, prophecy and the Word. We are becoming more and more one and Jesus is our center. The world is learning that Jesus came from His Father to offer any who would come to Him the whole kingdom and a new relationship with God as our loving Father. We are also becoming more aware of the enemy than ever before and the Lord is teaching us to be prepared and to walk in a new authority as sons that we've not experienced often before. He's beginning to show us glimpses again of what's ahead. We are now a stronger, bolder people, many of whom have been brought through a fire, who have been laid upon the threshing floor, who have been sifted out. We are being restored, vindicated, armed. So many pastors and strong Christian people I have known in the last year have been reduced, decreased, purged, refined, attacked, momentarily quieted. They are now emerging again strong men and women of God with a new authority. They are a united Christian body and again a people who can more easily praise, more easily speak truth. They are filled with new depths of wisdom, can be silent and listen to what the Spirit is saying, can more quickly repent, can easily weep and laugh. They are determined and committed. They thirst for righteousness. They can forgive themselves. They can rest in His Spirit. They can love.

We are a people who know now beyond the shadow of any doubt that our Father loves us and intends to give the inheritance of His Son Jesus to mature sons and daughters who are unyielding in the faith. The day of the Lord is upon us. Come, Lord Jesus. Come.

Father, thank you for loving me. In Jesus, Amen.

PART III:

Unity of the Body of Christ in the World

10

The Capitol Hill Interaction Council—A Perspective of Christian Ministry

Jesus then said to them, "Truly, truly, I say to you, it was not Moses who gave you the bread from heaven; my Father gives you the true bread from heaven. For the bread of God is that which comes down from heaven, and gives life to the world." (John 6:32-33)

The Challenge

The Smith Hill-Chad Brown neighborhood of Providence is in the first concentric circle out of the center city and includes within its environs the beautiful white marble state capitol building and other various state offices, court buildings and supportive services. It also includes the federal housing projects of Chad Brown, Admiral Terrace, Sunset Village and Carroll Towers. The first two are populated almost entirely by blacks and the latter two by the elderly. There are three grammar schools, two public and one parochial, a middle school and within two miles of the center of the neighborhood are Rhode Island Junior College, Providence College, Rhode Island College, Rhode Island School of Design, Brown University, Johnson and Wales Junior College, and the University of Rhode Island extension services and night school. There are half a dozen gas stations, five bars, one bank, two liquor stores, two drugstores, nine restaurants, two lemonade stands, three major hospitals, a police training school, one large chain grocery store, a branch of the Providence Public Library, one funeral director, three florist shops, one hardware store, several boarded-up storefronts, eight churches, three parks, one

163

neighborhood health center, and approximately 16,000 people. There are miles of streets and sidewalks, rows of old, three-decker, wooden houses, a fair number of trees, a few yards, lots of dogs and cats, constant litter, an unusual amount of wind, cold winters and hot summers. Two city councilmen, one house representative, and one senator, along with ward committeemen, represent our political district of the twelfth Ward which has traditionally been Democratic almost without challenge. When OEO fielded neighborhood resource units, Smith Hill-Chad Brown was classified as a number-one priority target area. In large proportions the neighborhood is populated by the Irish, Armenians, Lithuanians, Latin Americans, Italians, Scotch-Irish—blacks, whites and browns. There are smaller numbers of Dutch, English, Filipino, Laotian, Indian and German people. There are more ghetto streets and pockets than integrated sections. The majority of people are blue-collar workers although there is a surprising number of professional people. There is a very large proportion of people who are not working and, therefore, they are receiving aid. Incidents of crime, poor school attendance, alcoholism and venereal disease are high. Drug addiction is alarmingly high. Last year many of us were astonished at Christmas time to read that an organized crime hit man had been found in the trunk of his car with five bullet holes in his head. His address read two blocks down on the street next to our home. Only a week later we read of simultaneous FBI raids on seven locations throughout the United States to secure gambling books and receipts from the files of organized crime to begin what the papers said would be a long, arduous road to break the syndicate gambling operation in this country. Two of the seven raids were conducted in our neighborhood, only a few blocks away. The eight churches are: St. Patrick's Roman Catholic Church, the largest; St. Sahag and St. Mesrob Armenian Apostolic Orthodox Church, coming in a close second and servicing the whole state as well as our neighborhood; St. John's Episcopal Cathedral with a congregation, for all intents and purposes, outside the neighborhood, as well as Gloria Dei Lutheran Church. Along with St. Patrick's, St. Sahag and St. Mesrob with congregations by and large from the neighborhood are St. Casimer's National Lithuanian Church with members only from Lithuania, Iglesia Pentecostal with members of Spanish descent only, the United Baptist Church of the American Baptist Convention, and the United Presbyterian Church from the United Presbyterian Church of the United States of America. The last four churches perhaps total 400 members, with two of them limiting their membership to national origins. The middle two churches perhaps draw 600 between them but of these less than twenty members live in the neighborhood. The first two churches mentioned total thousands on their rolls but probably have between them 1,500 active participants, St. Patrick's being largely due to the charismatic renewal. Total active Christians? Perhaps 2,000 at best of the 16,000 people who live next-door to us.

At times I would be startled by situations I ran into. I became acquainted with one teen-age boy who had never heard of Jesus. He wondered who I was talking about when His name was brought up in conversation, and he became genuinely interested about this person who lived so long ago. I've found many other youth, tough in the ways of the street, who read the Word for the first time and became excited about what it said.

One elderly man we learned of because the rescue squad had been called for him. He had broken his leg while trying to carry a fifty-pound chunk of ice up to the icebox of his third floor apartment—he had no refrigerator. The ice had slipped and fallen on his leg. We discovered other elderly people who were unable to get out and would not see any other person for weeks on end. The only contact they would have with people at all would occur when an aide would deliver food stamps and then take those stamps to buy food the person wanted or when a district health nurse would check in. I found many elderly couples who had literally never gone out of the neighborhood even for trips or visits anywhere. Most of these had not purchased cars when the automobile replaced the horse and buggy. They had walked to stores at hand for their needs. I also ran across an attitude in most of the teen-agers that they would never move out of the neighborhood, probably would not finish high school but would marry, have children, work, have a few friends, hang around the street corners, and die. We discovered other people, young and old alike, who for lack of money couldn't buy fuel and who would live as best they could—bundled up in coats and blankets in apartments that didn't get above thirty degrees all winter.

Because of the hospitals being so close to where we live, we became used to the ambulances and rescue squad trucks racing by with sirens going full blast any time of the day or night. We have never been able, however, to get used to the police cars doing the same thing on an average of three or four times a night.

Racial tensions have always been evident. At their worst there would be flare-ups, especially with the children of the middle school near us. Again we live on the main route to school and frequently we would see periodic patrols walk by of two police officers, with shepherd dogs by their sides and guns in their hands.

Hundreds of times I have seen young men, with beer bottles in hand, urinating in the street or in our front yard. Occasionally we see a woman squatting to do the same. It is not infrequent when we go in to clean up apartments to find that the living room or the kitchen has served as the dog's or cat's or human's bathroom.

Stories like these could fill the pages of their own book and I'm sure they aren't uncommon to the heart of any city. This was and is our challenge. I still wonder what happens to the sensitive mind and heart in the midst of all this, lifting up its muffled, muted cry for life. When is it that we reach the turning point and no longer think of such things as human dignity or a life of peace and tranquility or the beauty of a baby's cry? When do we stop caring that there's a bird singing a song in the tree close by or a child looking up and watching what we do, intently listening to what we say? When does it happen that anger, violence, foul words and public displays of very private things become commonplace? And, conversely, when does the mind and heart finally say: "Enough! For me I shall search out the sanctity of life and find it even here in this hole of hell."

The Vision

As we took up residence in Providence and became increasingly aware of the downward momentum of life around us and as my own political and social views solidified, I became totally committed to certain axioms of life in the political, social, and economic spheres. Undergirding all of this was my Christian faith and Jesus was the motivator behind me in all that was to take place. It was a simple approach from His command to love others, for that's where He was and I wanted to be there with Him too. We cannot truly say we love Him if we can't love our neighbor. Loving our neighbor means feeding the poor, clothing the naked, bringing dignity to life where it has been lost. We would, though yet sinful, take our Christian blessing into the street where people lay starving for the bread of life, in the pit of their hungry stomachs, in the ravages of their emaciated souls, in the starved sense of their human dignity. Life should have integrity and purpose and we believed it still could in spite of the odds.

Socially, I believed in the integration of races, of ages, of ethnic backgrounds, of people, of wealth.

Economically, I believed in a more equal distribution of wealth. I felt it was incumbent upon those with wealth to realistically share their cup of blessing. Parenthetically, this became for me, however, a localized view; I believed we should be able to depend upon one another in our neighborhood for the sharing of resources while conversely depending less and less upon welfare systems which have, by and large, been abused and abusive, by and to people admittedly in need but then who find their need unnecessarily perpetuated. It's an ugly paradox that welfare is both a system of benevolence and a weapon of the rich to kill incentive in the poor. Many times thankful that government money paid for prescriptions or hospitalizations or food stamps or aid to dependent children or rental subsidies, I also have fought as hard as I know how for the change in thinking, and attitudes, and sometimes actuality that we must forever and a day be dependent upon these systems. There is more wisdom in building incentives, purpose, and ways in which we can help, one to one, and pulling each other up together into greater self-reliance.

Politically, I believed in democracy and the greatest amount of participation possible on the part of the people. Here I would like to mention as an aside what I still believe to be a critical ingredient out of my own experience. I, like most Americans, felt the alienation and disenfranchisement from our national government which was so rampant in the sixties and early seventies with the progression of the Vietnam War, the extension into Cambodia, the Watergate hearings, etc. To a lesser degree, I felt the same disenfranchisement from other systems of government such as those at state and city levels as well as national church structures. Though radically interested (we watched almost all the Senate Foreign Relations Committee hearings and most of the Watergate hearings), it produced in me more and more anger, frustration, bitterness and pain—all toward the conviction that my voice screamed out in the wilderness only to be heard by the rocks and sand. The more I realized this, the more untenable the whole situation seemed; the more I could relate to the poor people in the streets around me who had long before me become alienated from the larger structures which dramatically influenced their lives, and the more radically committed I became toward the realistic workings of democracy but in a setting relative to our limitations. The historic documents of this country are still unequaled in truth, wisdom, reality and dignity of government and the social life of her citizens, but these documents mean little or nothing unless they are alive in each and every small neighborhood and town of this country. The best way for our senators, congressmen, presidents and even our state representatives to hear about and then to live themselves lives of integrity, honesty, and statesmanship is for them to see in their electorate the lives of people transformed and positive, renewed and loving, caring and whole. There is no greater accountability for any of us than that of loving, honest, positive friends right within our vision nor any greater impetus to statesmanship than the knowledge of people at home who are desperately trying, right where they are, to improve their lot together with that of their neighbor. If democracy is to work, if social justice is to work, if economic fairness and promise is to work, it must work in Smith Hill-Chad Brown (the Capitol Hill area of Providence). Washington can only provide the channels for it to work better. Our job is not nearly so much being critical of our elected officials as it is living the very best of life we know how right in our own homes and for the people next-door. If, by virtue of our example, we have a hearing with any elected official, then count it as reward for the faithful stewardship of our political lives.

The vision? I found almost immediately that I was not alone in these thoughts. There was a strong number of people in the neighborhood who felt the same way and together we increasingly shared the hope that we could take the alienation, the frustration and hurt, the impoverishment of body, mind and soul, the separation of origins, the lack of purpose and participation, the fear and loneliness and turn it around. We did not have to nor would we accept defeat of what was good and right in the human spirit; rather we would lift it up—even for its own sake. It wasn't long before our concerns, Judy's, mine, and those of some other people in our church and from other churches and people in the neighborhood, became important enough to hold regular meetings and then to form a corporation as a vehicle of our concern. The Capitol Hill Interaction Council (CHIC) was born in the winter of 1969 and incorporated in the fall of 1970 as a non-profit, charitable corporation. By 1971 it began its long walk toward visibility and effectiveness in realizing the dream—a simple dream—that people could care for and help each other, that there could be dignity in life. From that day to this, United States senators and congressmen, governors, mayors, government economists and staff, policy aides, police chiefs, *The New York Times*, banks, religious publications, *The Providence Journal* newspaper, government health offices, numerous self-help institutions, attorney generals, bishops, councils of churches have heard about CHIC and have listened to what we have to say. More importantly, my neighbors next door are a part of CHIC.

Everyday Answers: the Thursday Luncheon

The meeting was over and we were talking on the street as many of the elders drove off. Peter Henry remained behind. Since the beginnings of CHIC, he and his wife Ella, Judy and I, and Peter's sister and brother-in-law, Mr. and Mrs. Kenneth Gilroy, were totally and actively committed to CHIC from our church. We had begun the previous year with a massive field day that included events ranging from cross-country races to three-legged races in the heat of the summer and during a time when racial conflict was high. We believed we could come together and enjoy each other in spite of hostilities on a hot day. I had remembered an example of this coming from the Ecumenical Institute in Chicago (an agency of the World Council of Churches) which believed the same thing and sponsored a huge picnic on their grounds in the midst of the ghetto on an equally hot summer day at the time of the Chicago riots in the late sixties. The difference? Their grounds were surrounded by National Guardsmen, holding rifles with bayonets attached, ten feet apart.

Our field day was different. We requested one plain-clothes detective from the Providence Police Force, who kept his gun holstered all day and enjoyed himself as much as we did. Over a thousand people came to enjoy, and not just a few to celebrate the belief we could indeed live together and enjoy one another no matter what color our skin was or what church we attended.

Peter mentioned to me that the church, during the war, used to have a chowder lunch every Friday for the hundreds of industrial and mill workers in our neighborhood. What about beginning another such luncheon? Peter was retired as was Ken, and their wives and they could help each week. The idea sounded good. The elders said yes, CHIC said yes and we began in May of 1971 to offer, each week, a luncheon which would provide a full-course meal, home cooked by different people, at $1.25. You could eat all you wanted to eat. Young and old alike were welcome. (We deeply desired to include everyone in this program, unlike the many senior citizens' meal programs that would be in a few years later and exclude anyone under sixty-five. We felt it was good for young and old to eat together, for a young person to hear a senior sing grace with a cracked voice and for a senior to hear a baby's cry or a youngster laugh.) It became the meeting place for many of the CHIC people and in this informal atmosphere we made plans and policies. It brought all the resource people of the neighborhood together and then, as time went on, it included all the resource people of the city and various government agencies that served our neighborhood. School principals, teachers, librarians, central library staff, pastors and priests, political officials, newspaper reporters, doctors, nurses, OEO staff, mayor's aides, directors of other community programs throughout the city, and others would often gather here for lunch and sharing, as would the poor, unwashed people of the neighborhood who held no other title than human being. For many years we enjoyed ethnic meals authentically prepared by people from particular ethnic origins. When we couldn't get someone for a particular day, then Peter and Ella or Ken and Catherine or Judy and I would fill in and cook our specialties. For three years we had help from a few ladies from one suburban church. As time went on we drew more consistent help from the neighborhood and Mrs. Greta O'Rourke finally took full responsiblity for the luncheon, cooked every delicious meal and for the last three years provided a joy for all involved. Prices were only raised once and then to $1.50. When the luncheon ended in late spring of 1978 that $1.50 meal would have been a $5.00 meal anywhere else. It was a unique experience of community fellowship where truly everyone great and small met and for a couple of hours each week graciously enjoyed fellowship.

Countless hundreds of times any leftover food would go to poor families so that never in the seven years was any food wasted. The numbers in attendance ranged from six to one hundred twenty and averaged around fifty-five. Only when a national holiday fell on the same day was the luncheon ever closed. When a person couldn't pay the $1.25 or $1.50 he could still come and be welcome. There were always others who would pay $2.00 or $2.50. In the very beginning the money the luncheon made was the only income for CHIC and from these humble beginnings of approximately $1,500 per year started the Shepherd's Staff, a full-time social service worker in Chad Brown and seed money for a youth organizer. But before all that another development took place.

The Butterfly

Believing innately in each person having a gift that another person would appreciate, Judy, with only a handful of other people, was inspired to open a handcraft self-development shop. With less than 100 items and a month's rent from CHIC for a storefront, they did so on January 15, 1972. Judy felt there were talents and resources in the neighborhood that lay dormant and craft skills, especially among the older women, that were dying out and needed new life and an impetus such as this to be shared and maintained in the younger generation. She also felt that selling handcrafted items meant more than a paycheck to the supplier. It was a matter of the spirit, that once a person's item sold it meant that someone else appreciated it enough either for themselves or for a gift for another they cared for, that the supplier would find new worth and value in life. Prices were always to be kept low enough that the poor as well as the less poor could afford nice things of handcrafted quality. Judy found help from the ladies in our church, the Baptist Church and the neighborhood in the beginning but now the shop also has men and women from St. Patrick's helping.

The concept immediately struck acceptance in CHIC where we firmly believed that the major resources to meet the major needs of our community were within our own community. Not only did the economic self-development reality hit home but perhaps more importantly the idea that something beautiful in spirit and quality was the very thing our neighborhood needed to start taking pride in itself again, to involve its people in positive growth, to chip away at apathy and loneliness. Judy, and a few others, picked the name—the Butterfly—because it represents a thing of beauty that emerges from a once-ugly cocoon. They also chose the name because it is an early Christian symbol of resurrection.

The Butterfly Shop has moved three times in order to keep on expanding. It has always paid for itself, has provided from six to ten thousand dollars a year to its suppliers, and has taken any money left over and contributed it to CHIC for its ongoing projects. Upon the last move of the Butterfly, the shop entered the CHIC building and now the rent the Butterfly pays goes toward the CHIC mortgage on its own building.

The handful of original suppliers has grown to a yearly average of 300. The original 100 items have been turned over thousands of times. Some of the people who volunteered to work in the shop in their first working experience have now gone on to paid positions elsewhere. Each year the shop trains a handful of CETA employees toward permanent employment. Always the Butterfly in a conspicuous storefront has brought a spirit of wholesomeness and beauty to its surroundings. Items from the Butterfly grace homes all over the world.

The management of the Butterfly is a coordinated effort of several people who work there. Since the years of its inception, Judy was the one who spearheaded this management and along with a few others volunteered hundreds of hours to make it work. Nancy Rougvie, Ella Henry, Catherine Gilroy, Edith Thornton (Rev. Edwin Thornton's wife) and Dorothy Gaskell were all close to Judy during those years and provided the kind of support that allowed the Butterfly to function and expand upon the original vision. Dorothy Gaskell was also my secretary in the church and a woman of quiet reserve, wisdom and insight. These gifts were not only valuable to me as Dorothy became a trusted friend and loving secretary but also to Judy as the Butterfly would experience changes from growth.

In 1976, Judy became increasingly aware that the time had come for her to step down from a leadership position and, though she would help and support the person who would replace her, she basically let go. She was sensitive to the need for the Butterfly to go through another stage of growth and that it could not happen under her direction. She prayed earnestly that the Lord would raise up the one who was to replace her. Ironically enough, it was not to be any of the people who had worked so hard with Judy in these beginning years to realize the first dream but an entirely new and fresh person, who would bring a whole new and exciting dimension and life to the Butterfly. As an aside here, it's interesting to watch the Lord work after such prayers are made and to see the difference in the way He will answer when it's a volunteer position as opposed to one that is paid. To be sure, it must be much harder for Him to raise up volunteers to lead other volunteers than those who will be paid. The whole community can also be assured, however, that in the one He has raised up, motivations are pure and the dedication of the person's work is one simply borne out of love.

Valerie Carleton was the one He would choose and who took

over as manager of the Butterfly in 1977. She brought, with her talents, a vision of improving the quality of the handcrafted items as well as a vision of improving the looks of the shop. She was committed to the thought that prices should reflect a sense of quality and integrity both for the person who made the item as well as the one who purchased it. Although this meant in some cases raising prices—a hard decision for the Butterfly in a poor neighborhood—it also carried the sense that things dedicated and made in the Lord had a priceless value in reflecting Him.

Many hours of Valerie's unselfish volunteer labor went into making this vision a reality. It was time for her gifts to be manifested in the continuation of the original dream. The Butterfly, as it was in the beginning, is still a little haven of joy, friendliness and hope and these fruits witness that there is hope to the bleak world and specifically to the drabness of Smith Hill life. The shop looks like and is as nice as any suburban or downtown outlet and it is a real source of pride for all of us.

Christmas in the Butterfly is a particularly joyful time. There is love and unity that neighbors share in as they come to do Christmas shopping. Valerie's smiling face radiates the joy of the season which continues for her all year around and her love for people is a gift for all who enter.

One example really tells the story best. It's not uncommon but it illustrates what can be done. Cecelia, an elderly lady, crochets warm slippers. Although she can crochet sometimes as many as twelve pairs a week she can never keep up with the demand. Her slippers have become known and not only are they appreciated by the average buyer but also by many people for whom they become the only footgear they can wear. Each month Cecelia receives a check that she very much needs to help pay her bills; the crocheting she has done has helped to keep her busy. The Butterfly has been an instrument of her happiness.

Some of the original people who started the Butterfly are no longer working there. Ella Henry died in 1973, a blow to us all. Equal to the church was the Butterfly community who came together in love during the time of Peter's bereavement to celebrate and thank God for her life. The Butterfly has changed with the new people who work there, but so it should, for only as it constantly emerges from its cocoon is the startling beauty of the human dignity it represents seen afresh.

The Shepherd's Staff

In the early spring of 1971, local OEO officials pulled back neighborhood resource units and CHIC was left in the position of handling neighborhood organizational problems and later social welfare services. We needed to begin small with very immediate concerns and were able with the proceeds of the luncheon to do three things: (1) We were able to pay a thirty-dollar-per-month stipend to Sister Janet LaDuke to work in the Chad Brown-Admiral Terrace black and elderly community; (2) We were able to rent a storefront for eighty-one dollars per month to house Janet's work, which eventually included a family service outreach counselor, the first state social worker in the state's second attempt in the last two decades to decentralize; and (3) We put together seed money that had been matched by funds from several churches and denominations to hire a full-time youth worker. These represented answers, however minimal and short-term, to the most pressing problems for us in the summer of 1971. The streets were still rocked with violence, the racial divisions between blacks and whites were severe and social services needed personnel.

The results of that summer are still being felt. Sister Janet, with the help of the housing administration of Chad Brown, and Kay Lovatt, one of CHIC's original organizers and a continual source of energy and inspiration to CHIC people, were able to organize the first viable tenants' association which has gone on to accomplish some seemingly impossible things on their own. They were granted through HUD, by their own persistent efforts, over three million dollars for renovations and new buildings. Our youth worker, James Gilbert, was able with his gentle and loving personality to build a strong rapport with the youth in the streets and to motivate many of them toward further schooling or employment. It was hard in those years, for many of the youth who were Vietnam veterans felt so alienated and alone that it had even become a major concern of the Veterans Administration and church denominations across the country. That Jim was able to steer so many of these young people into positive directions was a credit both to his ability and to his genuine loving concern. Our social services component was to grow. We named that first storefront the Shepherd's Staff because of the sense we had of Jesus' shepherding with His staff of life. He gave us the Bread of himself and did not want us to confuse it with physical bread. But He offered both in His love and asked us to do the same. For many people in our neighborhood, life would be completely untenable and unbearable if they did not receive aid and for them to be able to realistically self-develop would take much training and resources not immediately at our hands. The Shepherd's Staff has grown to three state social workers and two substance-abuse counselors through a special program of HEW in the validation of CHIC. Individual case files now number over 2,000. I've been proud of the social workers who have worked through CHIC as well as the two substance-abuse counselors, for they all share our deep concern for the dignity and worth of life. Each is there because of a deeper commitment to human values and each continues to be open. I thank the Lord for them, for each of them knows the work of the Shepherd in the streets and back alleys of His poor.

Our Daily Bread

Already mentioned was our time of worship together at Thanksgiving and of our distribution of food baskets. In a limited way in the past the Shepherd's Staff had food distribution capabilities year-round but it depended on our being able to sustain food drives and somehow we were never able to do that. But the idea remained and with the influx of the charismatic movement which was now also within CHIC, the idea took on proportions of vision. Now we knew with even greater determination that the Lord desired to feed His poor bountifully and well. In January and February of 1975 it was time to move. CHIC people met with other interested people in the neighborhood and from St. Patrick's to discuss food services. We met first in small groupings and no later than a month after our first small group meeting we were ready for anyone who was interested. In a larger meeting, over thirty came and we decided that night to begin a food cooperative rather than a soup kitchen, to elect a board of twelve and to charge that board with several responsibilities. Within another month CHIC rented still another storefront and on April 15, 1975, we opened Our Daily Bread Food Cooperative.

One man gave us the initial stock to start with as a seed to be paid back at cost on a monthly basis. That cost was $1,200 and it was paid back by the Co-op in one year.

CHIC is incorporated as a nonprofit corporation and classified by the IRS as a charitable organization. Under that classification we were awarded status on the basis of six to eight major categories which had to do with bringing harmony among racial-ethnic-religious varied backgrounds, bringing pride to the community, adding to the economic stability of the community, various service categories to the poor, various youth organizational activities, various housing concerns, and finally publishing our own newsletter or an equivalent. We were not to be politically involved in more than 10 percent of our activities and those had to be nonsectarian in nature. Indeed, they always have been nonsectarian and were it not for the occasional recorded support and a following letter to legislators for bills related specifically to the poor or occasional meetings to present unbiased political issues or candidates, CHIC has remained clear of any confusion. (Before CHIC had become incorporated the same group of people who were to incorporate began the Capitol Grenadiers Drum and Bugle Corps, a junior parade and competition corps. This became much of the model for us as we explained to the IRS in our status application our desire to build community pride, stability and harmony as well as positive activities for youth and adults—it was completely apolitical.) We also are bound in CHIC to maintain separation of church and state, and this came to be of special concern as we received more and more government funding for various operations. I say this here because no other one thing has caused graver concern than this nor has anything CHIC has ever done in other spheres of endeavor caused more confusion.

Let me begin with some of the confusions and express the different ways CHIC is viewed:

"THAT THEY MAY BE ONE"

1. *From the local Presbyterian church:* By and large, the members of the United Presbyterian Church have viewed CHIC as the major vehicle for their mission emphasis in the local community and have, as stated before, poured out their lives in the work and purpose of CHIC. So much an emphasis has it been, that there literally has not been much time left over to pursue other vehicles of outreach though CHIC has not exclusively demanded the time of all. Others have placed time and dollars in other places but the church's presence is most heavily felt in CHIC. Historically, this is very common for the Presbyterian church at large which has always viewed its mission as one integral with and in structures of the world; it has always been involved in influencing government and social structures by the presence of its people, and has always made strong statements and confessions concerning the social welfare of man being integral to his spiritual life. As the charismatic experience entered the lives of many of the people in the church, their understanding of mission and community did not change; it deepened and with even more zeal the people determined to serve the community (neighborhood) in which their church is found.

2. *From the Baptist church:* An almost identical stance was taken concerning CHIC. The Baptists, along with the Presbyterians, lamented our small mission capabilities and decided to join forces not only with us but with persons in the community who felt the same call toward the social gospel. The Baptists, if anything, viewed CHIC even more radically as totally a social institution and were less willing to live with the confusions that arose than were the Presbyterians.

3. *From St. Patrick's Church:* Beginning days found little or no confusion which only began when the St. Patrick's Word of God Community moved to Smith Hill. Now there were new definitions of community and mission. Understanding of community within the Word of God meant primarily community within the brotherhood of Christ, not neighborhood. Mission, though it was to all poor, was a vehicle for evangelization. Moving from these definitions meant that, by and large, CHIC could not be considered a mission thrust or quasi-ministry of St. Patrick's though they never discouraged any of their members from becoming involved if they felt so called. Because many did feel

called and became an active part of CHIC and tended to be more outspoken in their witness to Jesus, OEO local and regional offices took notice and we were twice involved in hearings trying to clarify for them our approach. In both cases they were satisfied that (a) in our second attempt as a newsletter, called the *Capitol Clarion,* where witnessing to Christ was a frequent item, it dealt with neighborhood news which couldn't exclude for us the mention of Christ; and (b) that funds CHIC funneled to Sports Galore, a St. Patrick's youth sports program, were not primarily used for evangelization but for sports.

4. *From news reporters:* CHIC is a highly spirited social agency with a peculiar amount of soul, an unusually high level of hope, a radical commitment to people, a joyful outreach to the impoverished, a baffling experience and nearly impossible to write about.

5. *From the community at large:* Less informed and less caring about such things, most of the community sees CHIC as a good thing, a stabilizing force and an organization with real heart feelings toward the people it seeks to serve. Norman Cabral, pharmacist across the street from the CHIC building, is a good example. Though Norman is not a member of CHIC, he is totally sympathetic with its program and his heart is one with CHIC's purposes. Norman himself is a wonderful witness of a man who cares for the people he associates with and sells to. He always goes beyond being a druggist, informing people about what they're taking, its side effects, etc., and is beloved by all. Just being in his store is a joy as he sets a tone of warmth and friendliness.

6. *From the CHIC board and membership itself:* Since its inception all meetings of CHIC have been opened with a moment of silence, sometimes a rather long one. Probably most of the board members pray to the Father through Jesus, a few may pray to Mary, a few may meditate, a few may daydream and perhaps, from time to time, each one's mind has wandered off toward home or the person next to them or the gravest concern of the day. Then meetings open to deal with anything from the mayor to litter on the streets, the traffic light on the corner to police brutality, the health center to schools, the old man next door to an agency of CHIC. Oftentimes

representatives from government, law enforcement, school department, health department, etc., are there to work with us. Oftentimes neighborhood people come to express their concerns or get involved. There can really be no confusion about CHIC as it serves all the people. It is not openly evangelizing. There is a moral and ethical commitment not to. The board has always understood its mission to serve the poor. Evangelization is the work of the church. Conversely, there is no government or social agency on this earth that can or has the right to bind the conscience of any man or tell him what he must or must not say to his neighbor. CHIC has always supported its members, its agencies and its representatives to speak as they see fit and many have seen fit to mention that Jesus is the One who motivates them by the power of His Spirit, especially when they are asked. There has been one overwhelming fruit in this approach. CHIC is the only social agency in the city of Providence with a reputation and actual life record of being able to work with all people without hostility yet still seeking fairness and justice for all. This has included policemen and their chiefs, politicians, businessmen, landlords, as well as the abused, the hurting, and the victims. I believe this happens not only because the ideal of CHIC is a radical commitment to integrity and dignity of human life but also because her people know that Jesus poured out only compassion and love to the sinner and he counted them all precious. In the beginning of organization, CHIC people in 1970 decided forthrightly that the means they would choose toward advocacy in any concern must reflect the desired ends and both of those were love—otherwise the way would be entangled with controversy and pain. We never saw achievement of a loving end as possible by means of hurting people in achieving it. Justice would still prevail and though it has always taken longer to achieve and has not always been too dramatic in process, the permanence of justice by loving means has been a profound fruit. This belief is surely found and deeply grounded in Jesus Christ and is only carried out when He is allowed to give the patience and humility it takes to achieve.

I mention all this here because I believe it has crucial bearing on the way Christians approach the world in these next few years.

There is yet a seventh way to view CHIC as do many of those who claim the baptism of the Spirit, who are vocal of their born-again nature in Christ, and who are an integral part of CHIC. They speak little of this view yet you can tell by the way they live that it lies deep in their spirit. They are a people who believe in unity; who work day in and day out serving the poor, washing their feet and cleaning up their vomit if need be, but significantly they do it side by side with their Christian brother and sister from another church. CHIC ironically is the vehicle where this can happen, where all the exhortations of our Lord concerning the final judgment in Matthew 25 are worked out by the righteous. These are the people with a new vision, who march to the beat of the Spirit of God who calls His body together out of weeping and mourning. CHIC is the vehicle now because there is no other structure accommodating this radical call, not even the churches. Evangelism will happen because the body of Christ is together but it will happen also because the world simply sees it written on the faces of the people and says, "See them, how they love one another," and it will ask why; and it will not be disappointed.

The Food Cooperative is perhaps the best example of all the CHIC agencies that operates this way. From its very beginning, like the Butterfly, it has been upheld in prayer by the people involved. Dennis DeLude, the first manager from those early days in April, 1975 until this last spring of 1978, is deeply entrenched in the renewal and saw this work as the eldership of his young life. He did not move without seeking the Lord, was gifted not only with an abundance of the Lord's joy but also tremendous wisdom and discernment. And Dennis was mature enough to act upon the wisdom the Lord had provided him. There were many occasions that Dennis had opportunity to directly mention the name of Christ and did not but would rather listen, affirm and love. When it was right and prompted by the Spirit, he was equally ready to speak about his Lord. I know of many who opened their hearts to Jesus for the first time in and through the co-op but for those who are not ready, there is no judgment or intimidation; only a loving service and smile. The co-op is the old cracker barrel gathering place of the residents of the Hill and hundreds of people are simply drawn there; ostensibly to buy food but few ever walk out the doors without having been fed deeply within.

The new manager now is Dan Nabor, a man of overwhelming peace and serenity in his Lord, whose very presence suggests Jesus gently walking beside the Sea of Galilee teaching His disciples, a man whose words about the Lord can easily bring tears of healing and a lifting of the spirit. Dan inherits a 1,000-unit membership again including the highest state, federal and city elected officials as well as the people who live next door to the co-op, a $2 yearly membership fee, a voluntary work requirement rather than one imposed for membership, a 9 percent markup, a savings margin between 17-50 percent depending upon what members buy, a bookkeeping system that tells him any hour of any day the total picture at that time of operation, one CETA position, between 50-100 volunteers at any given time, an excellent rapport with food suppliers, adequate shelf space and a quarter of a million dollars a year in gross sales.

Dan also inherits an unusual precedent. Because CHIC is nonprofit, it is eligible to apply for government funding, for private and corporate grants, for CETA training positions, etc. Also due to the heavy church involvement and commitment in our neighborhood both from charismatic and noncharismatic sources, as well as many people from the community itself, there is very little that cannot be accomplished. With proper direction, leadership and vision there really is not one business enterprise that cannot be started and with an intermingling of self-development and cooperative concepts in operation, not be a success with a high degree of permanence. This becomes an immediate problem for local businessmen. Because of their overhead, they must charge higher prices. The problem then passes on to CHIC and its high percentage of Christian membership. For a community to flourish with its time-worn institutions healthy and strong, small business has to be stable and making reasonable profits. Time and again CHIC has put its shoulder to the grindstone of organizing the businessmen's association without success until last spring when George Bradley, then-acting director of CHIC, was able, through his own competent and dedicated leadership, to draw them together for very positive ends. Previously all that we were able to accomplish was to help get greater police protection, a hollow victory for all of us. Now there is talk of making improvements for which we all rejoice. I think it is the Lord saying, "Well done, Christian servants. You heard my call of righteousness and were faithful." The co-op board had made two astounding decisions. Although they could sell fresh fruit and vegetables cheaper (and sometimes give it away from the donations of Christian farmers) than the fruit market across the street and two doors down, they decided not to. They worked with the manager of the fruit market who has been on the Hill much longer than CHIC and the result was that the co-op would send their membership there with a 10 percent cut in prices for the membership. The second decision was even more unusual. The meat market and grocery store three doors down from the fruit market, also on the Hill for many years, had been forced to close. Admittedly prices there were considerably higher but this had happened before the co-op was a viable force as it is now and although the co-op undoubtedly was one reason, it was not the only one. After some hostile feelings were aired against CHIC's use of CETA and the government's even having such programs, there began more positive thoughts of reopening. Many weeks down the road after this came the co-op's decision to lower the other market's overhead by supplying some volunteer help out of her membership. And the co-op would not pursue the selling of fresh meats. One week after this decision was mutually agreed upon and one week prior to the scheduled reopening, the market building burned with only a shell left.

The Lord is determined to help His poor. He is equally determined to do so with integrity and nonviolence to the total communities in which they live. This unity within Him is often a paradox to us but I believe He is also providing a way through the darkness. We must be one with His Spirit as it is now poured out upon all flesh. There is no other way. This is part of the newness of the age to come and it is uncharted for us as yet. We are moving into days of darkness and the darkness will be total. The only light will come from His Spirit both from within and without, but we will see His Spirit in ways to which we are not accustomed. We now walk into an age where the Spirit has been poured out on *all* flesh. We must learn new ways of perception. They are not a little bit involved with unity.

For right now in this section concerning the co-op, I believe the Lord led the way by the light of His Spirit toward two things: (1) deflation of prices for His poor; and (2) the dealing with the victims of that deflation with integrity and righteousness—still seeking unity, for His Spirit *is* there too. This story is just beginning.

Even more involved in this new walk now is CHIC's organ of publication and news dissemination.

The Capitol Letter

This is CHIC's third attempt at publishing and each attempt has been expressive of the vision and growth CHIC had at the time. The first was a very high quality tabloid printed newspaper filled with vision, and neighborhood news and issues. Its cost was basically borne by CHIC with minimal advertising, a volunteer staff, and was begun shortly after CHIC's incorporation and published when funds were available. The second was a series of mimeo sheets folded in half and stapled, published and worked out of a CHIC-rented storefront with full-time volunteer coverage and staff, including neighborhood news with large portions of Christian writing, much lower cost again borne basically by CHIC with minimal advertising, published weekly without fail and was begun midway in CHIC's now nine years of life from seed thought to today. Both publications were called the *Capitol Clarion*. As this second attempt was about to cease, CHIC was on the verge of making dramatic changes and policy shifts.

It was at this time under the leadership of Helen Hawkinson, the CHIC president, that CHIC began negotiating the purchase of its own building. Space was being rented in storefronts now for all the CHIC agencies and was amounting to $4,000 a year. Helen pursued several possibilities and finally presented CHIC with the decision of buying and moving across the street from their long row of storefronts, a huge 4½-story Victorian building with commanding presence on the Hill. The decision was affirmed and, in time, all the CHIC agencies decided to move into the building. Also up to this time CHIC was almost without exception a volunteer organization with a firm commitment to starting enterprises that would eventually self-develop and would not depend upon outside funding for their life. Helen encouraged the CHIC board to be open to new possibilities and under her dedicated and gifted leadership brought many new and vital services to the poor of our neighborhood. A funded executive staff was also initiated and Robert Nigohosian was hired as CHIC's first executive director. Though Bob and Helen have both gone on to new challenges, together they gave their lives to CHIC that it might follow its radical call to love people in ever-dynamic and imaginative ways. Through their superior dedication and long hours of work they were both responsible for moving CHIC into its present position as a dynamic recognized force for the good of all people. CHIC and her agencies are now the stewards of one-half million dollars yearly and a glass house visibility for both the rights and the real life of man.

While Bob was still the executive director, the third and present CHIC attempt at publishing came into being. The *Capitol Letter* is entirely different from its two predecessors and it's more aptly described as a journal publication on community living. It reflects its editor as did the first two publications. Thomas Carleton is a man of many faces who wears many hats. Tom is a gentle, affectionate loving man particularly sensitive to the hurts and pains of the world's downtrodden. Tom has worked most recently for the Urban League of Rhode Island in publishing their journal and in writing a film script depicting present-day life of the Narragansett Indians. Tom now works for New Life Enterprises, the subject of the next chapter. Tom and his wife, Valerie, and their newborn son bought an old home in Smith Hill which they are in the process of renovating. Tom and Valerie are also directors of Earthrise, Inc., a nonprofit futurist corporation for educational and scientific research into viable life modes of the future. Through Earthrise, Tom and his colleagues have designed a futurist game called

"Global Futures" in which participants learn to cooperate with one another for survival. Tom has presented this game with his slide lecture to universities and high schools throughout the United States and for the Hawaii State Commission on the Year 2000. Along with teaching responsibilities at the Rhode Island School of Design, Tom has also been an instructor in the University Without Walls. He is a professional graphics designer, an architectural designer, a conscientious objector to war after serving several years in the Marine Corps Reserves and is a Christian. I write all this about Tom not only because he is a very good friend of ours and someone we deeply respect, but in praise to God for His constant bringing of the right people at the right time not only into my life but into the life of the community of His people. All the names mentioned in the book and hundreds of others unmentioned were His people not only there for me to be loved by or to love but to prophetically prepare His way for all of His people. Truly, there are no coincidences with the Lord nor is there ever anyone we meet or know who He has not lovingly placed in our path.

The *Capitol Letter* is a journal-styled newsletter designed to do primarily two things: (1) to help the people of the Smith Hill-Chad Brown Capitol district of Providence live a more integrated, positive, fruitful, productive life in the environs of the dehumanized inner city; and (2) to share the experiment of community living out of Smith Hill-Chad Brown among other inner city groups attempting to meet the future from an urban base by way of shared information. Like its predecessors, the *Capitol Letter* is paid for by CHIC although this time, selected, limited advertising has been able to pay for the operational costs. The *Letter* is put together again by a volunteer staff, this time housed in the CHIC building and with professionals in the fields of graphics, photography, fine arts and journalism. Published bimonthly, the *Letter* is free of charge. While some 400 issues of each printing are sent throughout the country and overseas, the remaining 1,600 are circulated on the Hill. Tom shares all the concerns of CHIC as well as the Christian movement of caring upon the Hill. He also brings a fresh approach and some very realistic answers to problems in the urban setting. Familiar with problem solving in the fields of ecology and energy conservation especially as they relate to human values, Tom is opening new visions for all of us and, I believe, speaks prophetically as he shares his views of an emerging paradigm of hope, where human values are important over and above the complex seat of corporate, industrial, mechanized, computerized, governmental, conglomerate powers, in which the people have little or no input toward determining their future. I would like to quote from his lecture here various points which have challenged us beyond any of our previous thinking:

I believe that there is a significant change taking place today within our American society and elsewhere in the world. It is a shift in values and behaviors. This has been called a "paradigm shift." Paradigm is an important word to understand so let me define it for you. It comes from a Greek word meaning pattern. According to Ruben Nelson, director of the Cultural Paradigms Project in Canada, it refers to the taken-for-granted patterns of social, intellectual, emotional and physical organization by means of which the people of a culture or major subculture are formed and defined. A paradigm is a conceptual orientation of a people which results in our noticing some aspects of reality and ignoring others. It is the "knowledge" we live by. As mythologist Ken Davis has punned, "Buddy, can you paradigm?"

It follows from this that insofar as cultures have different conceptual orientations, they in some important sense do not live in the same world. My friend William Tutman claims that European-Americans, Asians and Africans differ in terms of the philosophical relationships they see as being important between humans and objects, nature, and other humans. Tutman says that European-Americans see the relationship between humans and objects as being the most significant. As you can see by looking around you, we have certainly created a materialistic society. In contrast, Asians have historically placed greater emphasis on the relationships between humans and their natural environment, while Africans have historically given higher priority to the relationships between humans and their fellow human beings. In my view, the

European-Americans have created a modern capitalist society that is exploitative and ecologically bankrupt and we have much to learn from our Asian and African neighbors to design a new world order that values ecological balance and social justice.

Now I think that you can see that there is a dominant set of values and behaviors in our society that could bring about a nightmarish future (described earlier in the lecture). There is also an emerging set of values and behaviors that could bring about a very different and I believe more desirable world. The dominant American paradigm, based on our Hellenic and European heritage, has seized control of the world's resources for hundreds of years. Earthrise co-founder Charlie Wolf and his colleagues have identified a range of characteristics to describe the dominant paradigm. I have selected and interpreted a number of these from my personal and professional experiences in a variety of organizations. Dominant institutions in our society can be said to be competitive, homogeneous (dominated by white males), culture-insensitive (racistly arrogant and violent), elitist (decision making is dominated by those who are socially or economically privileged), value-free (personal hopes and aspirations are suppressed), rigid (divergent points of view and new ideas are not tolerated), and reductionist (problems are isolated from their broader social or environmental contexts).

In contrast, Charlie has identified another set of characteristics in what I call the emerging paradigm—one that I would like to see emerge. Again from Charlie's list, the emerging paradigm can be said to be cooperative, heterogeneous (involving women and Third World people), participatory (involving larger numbers of people in decision-making), culture-sensitive (white racism is reduced), value-sensitive (the legitimate aspirations of each individual and the value orientations of non-Western cultures are recognized), flexible (open to change), and holistic (problems are solved or transcended in light of their larger social and environmental contexts).

Every day I feel the stress of trying to operate in the emerging paradigm while dealing with individuals and institutions firmly entrenched in the dominant (and until the present "successful") paradigm. This paradigm conflicts has been the source of a great deal of personal anxiety in recent years. Yet I know I must find a balance to insure my spiritual and physical well-being because I expect the conflict between these two value orientations (not to mention other emerging and changing paradigms) to last through my lifetime.

James Dator, one of my favorite futurists in Hawaii, calls this view of the future "transformational." He depicts this as two growth curves. The lower curve climbs, levels off and then sharply declines (in an apocalyptic collapse) or levels off again (in a "steady-state" of equilibrium). A second curve rises out of the first and climbs further until it levels off for a time. The lower curve can be thought of as the dominant paradigm and the upper curve as the emerging one. The area where the two curves intersect can be thought of the present (the later half of the Twentieth Century). Ruben Nelson refers to our current situation as the "crisis of the inappropriate paradigm."

Although I have been reassured by respected futurists that the institutions in the dominant paradigm are crumbling, I do not believe that the emerging paradigm will come about by itself. It will take a lifetime commitment to hard work without any guarantees of success. Personally, I do not think that people can be forced from one world-view to another. I think that they must be attracted to a new world-view by demonstrating alternatives. In fact that was why Earthrise was formed, to seek practical ways of facilitating the paradigm shift, although we did not think of it in these terms when we started back in 1972.

In our discussions we speak of shared reliance, combined with self-reliance, where more and more of the necessities of our human life are produced by ourselves including energy, food, clothing and shelter. We share a sense of learning a less demanding life style by simplifying the various systems we now depend upon such as cars for all our transportation and televisions for all our entertainment. Energy shortages, brownouts, blackouts, cut food supplies, money shortages, inadequate housing all seem inevitable. The loss of particular freedoms would normally follow this kind of dilemma and it would hit particularly hard our dominant culture today which knows few if any restraints. There is no reason why we cannot prepare ourselves much better than we are now for a future that will be considerably more austere than our present style of living. One does not have to be a theologian or know the Word to see what lies ahead in our generation. There are many lessons of wisdom one learns as he works with the poor of this world, whatever their impoverishment may be—not the least of which is to walk with them in their daily lives and feel their pain and suffering which you may never have felt, and then know their hope which defies all reason but sustains the very foundation of life. Soon you are willing to let go of many frills, indeed, even some golden dreams, to discover rockbottom—what really matters in this life. The answers haven't changed in 2,000 years. They are as simple now as they were then. I thank God He first gave us the sense of adventure as we began to see the first century emerge into the twentieth. And now I thank Him that He is preparing us with an impenetrable hope and vision for the simplicity and austerity of life to come before it is a shocking surprise in the dark. And I thank Him for giving us His Spirit who alone will chart our course in the dark waters ahead, drawing us together not out of necessity, but out of love.

CHIC has done many other things too numerous to mention. I did write of the above because they are the ongoing, daily visible things which happen. These are the vehicles through which love has been shared with all who pass by. These are also the channels in which an incomparable daily dedication and devotion to the task at hand has found its place. There are not enough songs and ballads sung to those who always consistently and faithfully perform their tasks. It takes thousands of man-hours each week to fulfill CHIC's sensitivity to the ongoing needs at her doorstep. The majority of those hours are still unpaid or paid very little. They are dynamic hours, flexible in approach as they must be, but they are radically important, each one building upon the other until real needs are met by real solutions in days of much unreality. They are, indeed, hours inspired and motivated by the Holy Spirit of God for many who give them and who simply say, "Christ has called me to love my brother; here is a good place for me to do it with the gifts I have."

As this book is being concluded, we were informed that Providence was one of the twenty-two finalists in the All-American Cities Contest. The selection was based upon three groups in Providence who excelled in their vision and ability to realistically bring renewal into their sphere of influence. CHIC was one of the three Providence groups cited by those making the selection.

None of us realized as we began CHIC that the Lord would use it, as I believe He is in these days, as a unique prophetic voice of preparation for the days to come and as perhaps the most visible, if not only, place where His body is one on Capitol Hill.

The Holy Spirit and the World

CHIC is a bridge from the church to the world. Smith Hill is not much different from any other community in that the majority of people who live in the neighborhood are not church attenders and seldom if ever find their way into the church sanctuary. Christians today must reach out, unlike twenty and thirty years ago when people flocked to the churches. And furthermore, they must reach out in new and different ways. People in the world are frightened, confused, unloved, unable to love themselves, accustomed to violence and loneliness, living behind locked doors. A person would come, for instance, to buy food at the co-op or gifts at the Butterfly or even for counseling from CHIC's social services component but would be petrified upon entering the church and would present to a pastor or priest a much different person than to the neighbor next door.

There need to be innumerably more bridges built for Christians to walk over into the world, for there are too few now that are completed to the other side or that are not obstructed somewhere along the way or that really are built strong enough to stand over the chasm below. I would venture a guess as to why we are so reluctant: we too are afraid. Most of us came out of the world pretty deeply evangelized by it. Even those of us who were born and raised in the church have been riddled through by the power and life of the world. Few have learned deeply enough what it means to be in the world but not of the world.

Now, within the renewal movement there has been a growing awareness of our power and gifted nature as sons of God. Our pentecostal brothers have tried to share this with us for one-half a century and we scoffed at them, turned them back and grew in fear of them. They on the other hand shook the dust off their feet and in many cases became more than a judgment upon the church and fell into the trap of judging the church.

For the last several years the renewal has heard in almost every denomination, "Go home and love the brothers in your own church." At home, Christians have humbled themselves before their elders and bishops and pastors, following the call of God to bring life together, to flock together in unity, to meet often and pray constantly, to submit, to grow in patience, to endure, to turn the other cheek, to love the unlovable and return love for hatred and divisions. Familes have been called together, husbands and wives to become one, to take proper loving authority and responsibility over their children and for children to be obedient and submissive to their parents' authority.

A few have heard the call to larger unity in the body of Christ, that churches, prayer meetings, healing services, programs, music—ought to join together in oneness.

And yet in all this the people of God have been afraid. They have turned, we have turned, I have turned to what was easy, to be renewed in the things which I chose to be renewed in and so on down the line until God spoke a hurting, commanding word at Kansas City, a word directly out of His precious love for us because He can see ahead where we cannot.

We have not successfully built bridges because in our fear we backed off to do what was more comfortable (even as painful as that may have been). In many places it became so entrenched to go home and die in the church body we were a part of that we did just that—we died. The Lord's Spirit moved on and we were still dying. Others were moving out but we said, "But the Lord said . . . !" And we did not go—we had become too humble. I'm not mocking here. I truly mean we worked so hard at our own personal sanctification, our own church's body or prayer group body that we failed to see the cloud move out over other bodies, gathering them all together to build the bridge out into the world as one body of Christ. I believe we lacked two things: (1) a radical sense of Jesus' commission in Matthew 28; and (2) an innate sense of authority within ourselves. We've had gifts, we've had power but we've lacked authority. We've had community, we've had structure but we've lacked courage to go out into all the world preaching and baptizing in Jesus' name. The saints have been equipped for ministry, hundreds of thousands of Christians have been empowered by the Holy Spirit. We are being pushed on the land. We've been called to leave our land fortifications behind because they can no longer be useful to us. The cliff is too high to scale to the sea. We can either jump and walk on the water or build a bridge to safe harbor but we cannot stay where we are. We must no longer doubt that the Lord has given us all we need for the journey ahead—He has given us His gift of love—He has given us His gift of hope—He has given us His gift of faith—He has given us power now as the Sons of God to rise up, now is the time. He has given us unity—He has made us one, we are one; in Him there is no division in us—now is the time to rise up and shout to the wailing, pained-destroyed world—"Jesus is Lord."

God our Father has fulfilled Joel's prophecy. He has poured out His promised Holy Spirit on *all* flesh. Everything that moves and breathes and lives has been covered with the outpouring of God's Holy Spirit. And now, even now, is the day when our Father is answering Jesus' prayer of the night He was betrayed, "Father, make them one even as we are one." He has made us one and weeps and mourns that we have lacked the courage to stand up with His authority and say, "We are one." It is for Him to know why it is that in these days we have received and will receive the most ridicule and resistance from the very churches that have been our homes, our land fortifications, when we stand up and proclaim our oneness. That should not have stopped us but now it must not stop us.

He has blessed us to take away our fear. His Holy Spirit is in the world. It has gone before us. As we bridge to the world we will find Him again. As we jump in the sea to walk on water we will find Him. There is no more time to carefully plan a bridge for Presbyterians to cross, a bridge for Baptists to cross, a bridge for Roman Catholics to cross. We must cross any bridge available and we must go together. I'm convinced in the Spirit that as we go together and establish a beachhead on the other side we will see the most explosive revival, renewal, advance of Christendom the world has ever known. It may not look at all like past history, for the heavens are in preparation for new history and cataclysm no less powerful than the Advent and Incarnation, Crucifixion and Resurrection of Christ.

I believe the light will be with us no longer in ways we have been accustomed to. How often we would receive that passage from John 12:35-36, and not realize what it meant. I now believe it means that the light, even the presence of Christ, will much more deeply be perceived inwardly, that His outside presence which we've grown accustomed to will be gone, He will seem like a vague mist to the mind's eye but His Spirit, yes, the Holy Spirit will be a light within. The world will be in darkness. The children of the world called to be children of God will see a light emanating from us that even we are not aware of. It will carry with it a new authority and power, a present and immediate winsomeness. But we will need to be sensitive to new ways of perceiving and following the Spirit within.

Matt Steward, one of our elders in the church, believed perhaps more than any of the others that we would only enter this new age as Christian brothers together. He spoke often of the pain he experienced deep in his spirit over the brokenness in relationships he was acquainted with. Matt is gifted with an abundant amount of wisdom and often when we discussed our status of unity within the community, he would point out the half-truths we were all willing to live with. Matt felt his call was to evangelize and with three brothers from St. Patrick's he went weekly downtown in

Providence to share the Word with any who were interested. Matt would come back and relate to us incredible stories of how the Spirit would lead persons to them, begin conversations, and end up often opening the hearts of those sent to accept the Lord or asking for healing prayers. Matt and the three others were determined to be together and equally determined just to stand waiting for whomever the Lord would send—they never pushed their way on anyone. In time they were to notice that those who the Lord would send would emanate a different presence of their own that Matt and the others would "see" fifty feet away as the person would approach in the midst of scores of other people. Some nights many would come this way, some nights only one; occasionally none would come and it was on those nights that Matt and the others knew the Lord was about the work of drawing His body of four even more closely together, knit in every place into the sensitivity of one body.

Phil Sheridan, from the Wednesday Morning Group, began a Bible study in the spring of 1978 in the Smith Hill neighborhood. His firm and studious commitment to the Word of God has lead him to recognize the vacuum not only in communities but more importantly in churches concerning the Word and the radical need for Christians to derive their growing positiveness of faith and authority from it. Phil began with a handful of people and now a half year later the group numbers some 80 people. It's significant that these are people being raised up who have a deep hunger for the Word. But there are other things even more significant in conjunction with their hunger for the Bread of Life they find in the Word. They are first of all from every conceivable tradition and background and share a wide variety of Christian experiences. More importantly, many have had experiences in their lives with the various anti-Christian cults so numerous today as well as some with the occult. By the time they have reached Phil's group they are either dry and worn out or newly born into the Christian faith. In either case, they sense almost immediately their need to be fed and the Word provides their every meal. Many have another common interest, and it's music. They were either professional entertainers in the world of rock or amateurs at home but the Lord touched them and drew them out, quieted them and then began to fill them with songs and music straight out of the heavenly spheres. Phil's Bible study has already built significant bridges into the world and as he shares with us in our group, we are touched each time with an urgency that the needs are phenomenal; the world awaits and is filled with hungering, searching people; the Word and the Spirit are willing to provide the fullness of the banquet table; the people receive, grow, become equipped, gain wisdom and go out with a previously unwitnessed, unprecedented haste. Every time they cross the bridge they find more. They go together. Time is short. Awake, O sleeper, for the time is now. We are entering a new age. Do not miss the fullness of joy the Lord has prepared for us all.

O Lord, I thank you for all those whom you are raising up in these days to witness in love without judgment to your outpouring love as it seeks to touch every corner of the world. Thank you for erasing the distinctions that have separated us in the past, for the Spirit in the world, for the ever-increasing awareness of the light of Jesus Christ, for the power, discernment, and love to work through whatever structures are available to show forth the one body of Christ, for your guiding hand in all our past experiences and ventures. Father, prepare us for the days ahead through Jesus Christ our Lord. Amen.

11

New Life Enterprises—
A City Set on a Hill

So the wall was finished on the twenty-fifth day of the month Elul, in fifty-two days. And when all our enemies heard of it, all the nations round about us were afraid and fell greatly in their own esteem; for they perceived that this work had been accomplished with the help of our God. (Neh. 6:15-16)

The brilliant array of those who worship God in heaven, as depicted in Revelation 4, "never cease to sing, 'Holy, holy, holy, is the Lord God Almighty, who was and is and is to come!' And whenever the living creatures give glory and honor and thanks to him who is seated on the throne, who lives for ever and ever, the twenty-four elders fall down before him who is seated on the throne and worship him who lives for ever and ever; they cast their crowns before the throne, singing, 'Worthy art thou, our Lord and God, to receive glory and honor and power, for thou didst create all things, and by thy will they existed and were created' " (Rev. 4:8b-11).

It seemed upon my pending resignation from the pastorate of the United Presbyterian Church, with no church call in hand, that the Lord was indeed preparing a way for me to walk that would be yet a glory to Him, that would not be a way of striving out of a lack of peacefulness but one which would provide abundantly, that would proceed with vision and prophecy, that would show forth the crown of life at His feet proclaiming Him worthy, for indeed He did create this new path and ministry. It seemed that out of the traversing of hell from which He was lifting me it was right to proceed in faith and to take the step of faith onto the water ahead and walk. He would provide if I was willing again to surrender, for His covenant with me was unbroken from His point of view. Again, I remembered the quietness and beauty of the field lily which praised Him merely in its being and began expectantly to look for His guidance. As it developed from very simple truths and needs, He guided me and a small group of friends into an incorporation titled "New Life Enterprises." The papers and documents of the corporation concisely set forth the simple goals toward which we have committed our lives and the assumptions upon which we selected our goals. For my own part, I began to assume with a new freedom some very simple things; for instance, that it was no longer wrong to have friends and unabashedly admit I needed friends. I no longer wanted to live in an aloof pastoral role which negated special friendships. I made theological assumptions. If indeed His Spirit is being poured out on all flesh in fulfillment of Joel's prophecy (and I believe it is), then His Spirit will be found everywhere, not just in the visible church and that I was being led to build a bridge between the church and His Spirit in the world. I was also led to conclude that this was to be done without anxiety and financial stress—that as we faithfully follow Him, He will truly bless us with all we need. This meant for us the development of self-realization through shared reliance in our incorporated efforts. It meant that we could share together not only in friendship but materially as well so that in a very real sense, we would be in pursuit of first-century Christian community where life and possessions were shared in common for the benefit of all. It also seemed well at this point to share our lives honestly with one another and to remove all pretentions and masks, to speak honestly about our frustrations and disappointments even and especially with one another and to finally submit our lives to each other and more deeply the Lord in each other. We set out to live Christian community.

New Life Enterprises was incorporated May 1, 1978, after four months of planning and fellowshiping with fifteen shareholders as a profit business with multiple enterprises under one umbrella. We determined that there were over fifty enterprises we might endeavor to accomplish according to the various talents and gifts of the fifteen shareholders and that some of these were desirable from the point of view that a shareholder or group of shareholders together might want to pursue a latent talent that they never had the time or resources to accomplish, that this might well be the talent the Lord wanted them to employ and that as they did, He would bless it for the whole as we joined the resources of the corporation together behind our fellows' latent talents.

It soon became apparent that the Lord gave us a very practical task and vision. On May 1, I began working full-time in New Life. Judy, along with all her household tasks, began working part-time. Martin Mijal, who had just received his master's degree in counseling, decided also to work full-time for New Life beginning May 1. Dan Novak, student advisor and instructor in philosophy at the University Without Walls decided to work full-time in June. John Watkins, interim pastor of the United Presbyterian Church who replaced me in the pulpit, decided to work part-time in July. John's wife, Anita, decided to work part-time in tasks oriented to her skills. With all this we needed to generate and produce income. The Lord led us directly and quickly into home renovation with particular emphasis on exterior painting in the summer months. We were to prepare the foundation for interior renovation by the fall when Tom Carleton would begin working part-time, his wife, Valerie, part-time, and the possibility of Ron Scopel, social worker, full-time. We also laid plans for Matt Steward, optician, to potentially begin in the fall. This planning all required an upward wage scale from minimum wage, where we all started, to five dollars an hour by November, 1978, which everyone felt they needed to maintain support while helping one another through the rough times. As the work grew, we began to sense a real forward purpose in restoring the city walls. We found ourselves painting many of the houses in our neighborhood and with this sense of purpose, we committed our lives and the corporation to integrity in our work. We desired to realize only a ten percent profit on our work and we would not cut corners as we discovered painters can easily do. In reading Nehemiah, we knew there would be an enemy and indeed there was, for as we made our commitment to integrity we began to lose production and at one point in September we were informed by our treasurer, Pat Hayes, who was retired from the business world of opening food chain stores, that we were in serious trouble financially. We had tried to learn all summer the balance between integrity work and being productively competitive, the balance between not overcharging any customer for loss on the previous job with reasonable fair profits for our labor on all work and had discovered the potential divisiveness of trying to achieve this balance. Pat's sober report brought us again into the unity we began with, called us to further sacrifice, and the Lord has blessed the simple fact that we told one another we were sorry for any division we had caused, asked each others' forgiveness and moved on with greater, more resolute purpose than before. We discovered a number of things. There can indeed be honesty and integrity in the business world while still realizing a fair profit. The Lord deeply blesses every move of integrity, every step of righteousness with some gift. Our unity in New Life is of peculiar importance and again we were all reminded of the subtle enemy of negativism which can so easily destroy a strong, positive approach and which needs to be properly combated each time it rears its ugly head. Much is lost both in the world and in the church when the majority of positive people walking in faith lack the courage to speak up and combat a negative suggestion, call it for what it is, recognize the real enemy behind it and lovingly but firmly and authoritatively dispel all negativity. We are, however, equally committed to encourage each shareholder to speak from his or her heart any feeling they have about any decision especially if it is negative so we can all look at it and deal with it openly. This is part and parcel of our shared unity and reliance upon one another.

We are guided by the vision the Lord has provided of restoration of the walls. CHIC and the churches have long desired and hoped for the visualizations of the inward renewal which has taken place in the hearts and minds of the people of Smith Hill but in the long years of their endeavor it has not happened. New Life is not alone in sensing now that it will be accomplished through the normal process of business, business which is guided by the Lord toward the end of the visual expression of His renewing Spirit. Toward this end, New Life has already replaced free of charge some boarded-up windows with a painted mural depicting renewal. We are also in the process of purchasing storefront buildings which we will restore and bring back to their original beauty. Our second exterior painting contract was with CHIC for their four-and-a-half-story building which was beautifully brought back to life, reminiscent of the Victorian era in which it was built.

Sharing the same vision as New Life, Ken Abrahms, a member of St. Patrick's Parish, left his job with the state as a professional painter the same time New Life started and in a step of courage and with the faith to walk on water, not unlike ours in New Life, he drew together a company with two other partners, Dennis DeLude, already mentioned as the previous manager of Our Daily Bread Food Cooperative, and Joe Pyres, previously an electrician on pole maintainance for the local electric utility. Ken, Dennis and Joe are all men of maturity in the Christian faith. They all have families to support and derive their well-being from hearing, trusting and then obeying the Lord. They share with us the same vision. We have exchanged workers on various jobs. We pray for one another. We share the same strong sense of integrity. Ken was the original impetus and teacher for us as we embarked on exterior painting for our first enterprise. The most interesting thing to watch in our relationship as two companies with identical purpose in the same neighborhood, however, is the way the Lord will share the same word with both of us and when we later share together the things we have learned, we rejoice to discover that we had learned the same things independently. There are also significant differences in our two operations that cause us to grow, stretch and learn.

We have found a distrusting and fearful world. For the most part, people do not trust us simply for who we are and although we know we are giving them honest work with a high degree of integrity, it must be proven to them, for they innately distrust the business world. Though we continually monitor our own accountability, many people feel the need to watch us at first. It has been this initial distrust that has 'ed to a positive witness, however, and before the work is completed, new friends are made. There is a particular fear among the elderly who are admittedly so vulnerable to the ploys of a dishonest business world. We have discovered the bidding system, under which we labor, to be one which is built up in all its nuances upon a system of distrust and that practically no one will allow you to work, believe in your internal accountability systems and then be charged for the labor by hours worked. Without a high or unusual degree of integrity, this will cause any company that lost on the previous bid because of either an inaccurate bid or greater work than anticipated, to pass that loss on to the next customer who will then pay more than what is fair for their work at hand. And in paying our initial premium to workman's compensation, we found that we had embarked on a particularly expensive enterprise for our first one, in that workman's compensation for painters is second highest only to steeplejacks because of the heights involved but also because of the unreliability of painters in general, much due to the problems of alcohol. Studies have shown that because of the conditions of weather being more determinative in exterior painting than in some other professions (the general principle being that uncontrollable forces determine work schedules) a more independent, free-wheeling type of person tends to take these kinds of jobs. Latent within such a personality is a need often expressed through alcoholism. At one point during the summer of 1978, New Life had four alcoholics on its work roster and the challenge of the Lord's desire to set free His children from such bondage was ever-present. Painting was only the vehicle for establishing relationships that were supportive and fulfilling. We also employed five Inter-Varsity college students in Providence for a work-study program for the summer. One image will always be indelibly impressed on my mind. As I returned from a bid one day to the work site I saw John Watkins (a good preacher and obviously earnest in season and out) standing on a second-story roof, arms gesturing sweepingly as he shared the Lord's good news with the alcoholics and Inter-Varsity young people together.

We believe as shareholders that the work experience in New Life ought to be supportive of and not detracting from the primary relationships that are before us. For many of us that means our families but for others who are unmarried it means any whom the Lord has called them to love. Again I assumed, as have many of the other shareholders, that in these days the Lord deeply desires for these relationships to be one—that they will be severely tested and tried, fired and refined until they are indeed one. Many of us had experienced in our traditional working relationship an insensitivity on the part of our employers whether the church or university, factory or school, to the increasing need for these first relationships the Lord has given us to be strong and equally filled with integrity and wholeness as our work. In practical terms this meant at least that we would be happy in our work. To a larger degree, the hope is that those relationships would find support among the community of people we chose to work with and that we would all be sensitive to one another's needs. Again, practically, this meant for many of us the freedom to pursue our giftedness or inclinations of talent under the relatively secure umbrella of New Life. As long as New Life moved as one unit, its shareholders were honest and in submission to one another, and trust was as highly valued as accountability, we could indeed pursue avenues yet unchallenged. To be satisfied in the work community meant all this and still one more actuality—that a working shareholder would be free to follow a varied work experience. For example, one day we might find ourselves painting a house, another day building a dollhouse, another day writing a book, another day taking our family to the beach, another day pursuing a whole new venture for ourselves or the corporation. All that was necessary basically was the scheduling of work ahead of time and the vow toward a more simplistic, uncluttered life style.

A good example of the nature of this is the writing of this book. As I sit writing even now, it is a New Life workday and the sun is out. It is a good day for painting but more pressing in my life right now is the deadline for this book. Last week on Monday I cut felt for banners. During the rest of the week I painted during the day (Judy joined me painting on Friday). We cut banners in the evenings and also planned the menu for New Life's next catering job. Saturday we relaxed. Sunday morning we worshiped in Jake's newly-appointed church and Sunday night joined him at Aaron's

Episcopal church where we participated in a healing service and I preached. New Life Enterprises has made this possible while the corporation made its fair profit last week. We all received a paycheck, invited each other to meals and enjoyed the life the Lord had given us. In the meantime, I had time to spend with my family, time that was relaxed and good.

The concept of unity finds its greatest blessing and curse in another guiding principle we assumed was right in the beginning of New Life. Each shareholder is also a director on the board. Many of us are also full-time employees but each has an equal share in the vision and movement of New Life decisions. The board confers particular authority to particular individual shareholders for specific projects for the sake of dispelling confusion. Otherwise, fifteen people make decisions mostly by consensus. It's definitely a harder road to travel but a road we believe is right and again as long as we employ the gifts the Lord gave us toward unity in His body it is a road festooned with garlands.

We believe in unity in New Life and that the greatest gifts of faith, hope and love will bring about that unity. It is not a unity that disparages truth or that does not desire to deal with truth honestly and openly. In that unity and with the emerging combination of self-determination and shared reliance, we hope to meet the future practically and victoriously. Spiritually, the Lord continues to lead us into simpler, more truthful and loving lives, committed to each other not only in work but in a myriad of other ways. We believe He is using us as one instrument toward the visual restoration of the place in which we live that it might show forth the city light set upon the hill and that it truly may be a healing balm to the nations both inwardly and outwardly. We believe the future is indeed our friend because it is the Lord's future but that the way is prepared not unlike John the Baptist preached—through repentance and works that befit repentance (Luke 3)—that mountains will be laid low, valleys filled, crooked roads made straight through our simple lives of integrity and righteousness. Every time we make a decision that is right, simply right in the Lord (for example, to support the relationship of a husband and wife toward greater oneness) He blesses us. We believe that any business enterprise can be undertaken honestly and still prosper and that we can effectively dispel the fear and mistrust we so often find in the world around us and set free in many little ways the children of God. And I firmly believe we are the church, building bridges into the world where the Spirit of God has been poured out, a world truly in travail and yearning for the sons of God to arise and take their proper place.

I remember a story from my youth. It was about Ben Franklin who, upon completion of the First Continental Congress, is said to have looked at the chair in which George Washington sat. He long gazed at the carved half-sun and rays emanating from it that was a part of the headrest of the chair. After a long pause, he commented that he was agonizing over whether it was a setting sun or a rising sun. He said he now believed it was the rising sun.

Likewise, our New Life emblem is the sunburst. For me it rises on the dawn of a new age.

Thank you, Father, for the promise of the continual new dawn, for learning how to work in various new ways, for your provision, for the precious gift of restoration, for the sure and certain promise of resurrection into new life ever vibrant and eternal. Father, I want to bless you; I want to be a good husband and father, a faithful son, a man of God reflecting your incredible love. I surrender myself to you again in deep thanksgiving. You have never once broken your covenant. You sealed it instead with the blood of Jesus—an innocent Lamb slain, your Son—that all of us might come to you free and unblemished. Father, help us to be one, that Jesus might reign in the hearts of all men. In His name we pray. Amen.

12

Conclusion

It was a beautiful day in May and one which we would all remember as much as the bride and groom. The church looked nice; it was resplendent with banners and freshly cut flowers; it had been decorated with the loving, tender, careful touch of the bride's family. Everyone invited to the wedding would be invited to the reception following in rooms off the sanctuary. I had turned over the pulpit to another Presbyterian minister and to a Catholic priest who were both to officiate at the wedding. The elders had discussed and then voted their concurrence with what was about to happen. (On one previous occasion, they had also discussed and voted concurrence in a matter of equal magnitude. Judy and I deeply desired to have Jake baptize our last child, Becky, shortly after her birth. We asked Jake and he wanted to as much as we desired to have him, so we submitted the request to the elders as he did to his bishop. The elders said yes; the bishop said no. We moved to compromise, as we had learned to do before. We felt that would express, as well as we knew how, the joy of our common love for Jesus and each other but which would still be obedient to present church authority. Jake preached and I baptized Becky and it was still a startling demonstration of love as the Lord again used a child to confound the world. My dad had also come to share in this special day; Becky was properly "signed, sealed and covenanted for the Lord's kingdom"; her parents and the congregation of her elders were properly charged with their responsibility to represent and be the Lord to her; and Jake preached a sensitive, loving and prophetic sermon.)

John and Anita were the groom and bride; John, a Presbyterian minister and, as already mentioned, my parish associate; Anita, a Roman Catholic laywoman. Several other Presbyterian ministers took part or were in the congregation and John's father, also a Presbyterian minister from Michigan, was to co-officiate with a Catholic priest who was a very dear friend of John and Anita. What made this unique was that the two clergymen concelebrated the sacrament of the Lord's Supper in one of the most tender, awesome and humble Communion services I've ever attended. We all walked up to the altar to receive first the bread and then the cup, one from each of the two participating clergymen. It was the first and only time I've ever attended or had anything to do with one table, one Lord, one body. I didn't know whether the roof would cave in, the earth tremble, the Lord speak audibly, tongues of fire descend or the whole assembly ascend to meet Him in the clouds. We have spent our lives in submission and although I've only known an open table in my own tradition, we painfully respected our deeply-loved Catholic brothers and sisters in their submission to their bishops. In the strictest sense, this unique Communion was out of order but I witness to this: the Lord was there; He was tender and loving and it was as though a protective shield had been wrapped around us all. He enclosed us all in His arms and blessed us. We wept and I knew in my heart and in my spirit that we blessed Him and He was pleased.

I've known the Lord to still bless many things that I've thought at the time were much less than what He must desire in His own heart. Though the body of His Son is still broken, He continues to bless each part; though a marriage might be bankrupt, He still blesses each partner. That doesn't mean things are right or that all things are according to His perfect will. I've witnessed Him so many times love right through the disobedient son, so many times

I've seen Him affirm the sinner. Indeed, some of the most beautiful times I've ever been with my Lord are those times when He has either loved me or another who was deeply in sin and at that very point of sin, convict while gently lifting up. He will not crush the already-bruised reed or blow out the weak, flickering wick. He will feed with His love. He will nurture with His tender, affectionate care. He will become one with us and die upon the cross.

Might this time not have been just like the meeting with Cornelius and Peter? If the elders had taken a vote would they have let Peter go to the house of this centurion? If Peter had had a bishop would he have said, "Yes, Peter, go with my blessing and complete the Lord's work"?

As trite and corny as it may sound, the sun did stream in at that very moment and shine in one brilliant ray upon the table and upon the bride and groom. There aren't many places for that to happen in our sanctuary nor many moments in the day when it's possible.

When I prayed to the Lord about even including this beautiful story in the pages of this book, I received two words. The first was this:

And they made a calf in those days, and offered a sacrifice to the idol and rejoiced in the works of their hands. But God turned and gave them over to worship the host of heaven, as it is written in the book of the prophets: "Did you offer to me slain beasts and sacrifices, forty years in the wilderness, O house of Israel? And you took up the tent of Moloch, and the star of the god Rephan, the figures which you made to worship; and I will remove you beyond Babylon." Our fathers had the tent of witness in the wilderness, even as he who spoke to Moses directed him to make it, according to the pattern that he had seen. Our fathers in turn brought it in with Joshua when they dispossessed the nations which God thrust out before our fathers. (Acts 7:41-45, from Stephen's sermon before the high priest and people before he was stoned to death.)

"Lord," I prayed, "was this time of sharing one table as one body the worship of the golden calf or was it the tent of witness? Is it so much my own desire that I'm deceived into thinking it's the desire of your Spirit?"

I turned again to the Scriptures and this is what I read through eyes filling with tears:

> *On the third day there was a marriage at Cana in Galilee, and the mother of Jesus was there; Jesus also was invited to the marriage, with his disciples. When the wine failed. . . . (John 2:1-3a)*

It was the tent of witness. Jesus did not harm the law, He fulfilled it in Spirit and love. He was there and it was right. He weeps that order has not caught up to His Spirit.

Christian unity? What really separates those who love Jesus, those He calls His brothers and sisters, those He has led into the kingdom of our Father? Surely it's not our Father who sent His Son to die. Satan? Only when we allow him does he have the power to divide us! Then the answer must rest with us who are the very family of God. We have authority as sons of God to dispel Satan because Jesus lives in us. We also have been given eyes to see and ears to hear the Lord Jesus in each other. There is a fullness in the family of God. I need Jesus in you and you need Jesus in me—Christ in us, the mystery of all ages—we desperately need the Lord in each other. He has given us the one gift necessary above all others to become the one family our Father intends us to be. He has given us love. Furthermore, it is a love empowered by the baptism in the Holy Spirit and strengthened with every other gift we allow the Spirit to give. Also it is a love that today is built upon the ashes of our Lord's refining fires, a love left as the wheat and chaff are sent up from the threshing floor and the chaff is blown away, a love that knows the forgiveness of Jesus and the gentle touch of our Shepherd-King. It is a love that can now speak truth in the genuineness of giving our lives to one another and saying, "I'm no longer embarrassed or compromised by the Lord in my brother and sister, no matter what their tradition. I'm proud of the Lord in them, just as I'm proud of the Lord in me, just as I'm proud of the Lord, even my blood-stained Jesus, hanging on the cross."

Christians, my brothers and sisters, hear the call! There is no time left, for our God has broken the seals. He intends to pour out His love upon the world in a way we've not known. It will be through us as one body of Christ. Our father is in too much pain over the broken, screaming world to wait any longer. He has only His family to work through now, for He has already poured out His Spirit upon us all, indeed upon all flesh. Now is the time for the sons of God to rise up—and to rise up as one. We don't even know what this kind of love will do to our bishops, pastors, elders who don't yet see because they also have never seen this kind of love. And we can't begin to dream of the impact upon the world our Father intends through the one body of Christ. We worship and love Jesus. Oh, we fail—yes, miserably; but we are restored, we are renewed—even like eagles— yes! We love Jesus because we know what He has done for us. Then let's listen hard to what He prayed:

That they may all be one; even as thou, Father, art in me, and I in thee, that they also may be in us, so that the world may believe that thou hast sent me. (John 17:21)

Appendix

The First New England Regional
Conference of Catholic Charismatics

Bishop Gelineau read to the 14,000 gathered participants a
telegram sent by Pope John Paul II expressing his warmest regards
and prayerful support on the occasion of the First New England
Catholic Charismatic Conference. It was the impetus for great
rejoicing and as it was being read there was a sense of the mighty
hand of God finally bearing a harvest of precious fruit borne
through obedience and faithful submission of literally thousands of
Catholic priests and laity of the Catholic Charismatic Renewal. It
has often been difficult for Protestants and pentecostals to
appreciate the degree of obedience and submission lived out among
their Roman Catholic brothers and sisters in these last ten years of
renewal but none of us can deny the fruits of the harvest. The Lord
has deeply rewarded the obedience of His people by touching their
leadership in an open and loving way. The significance of the papal
telegram is exciting and far reaching.

Not coincidentally, the themes of the conference dealt with new
beginnings. The participants loved Jesus as their Lord and Savior,
were filled with His Holy Spirit and empowered for a life of love
and servanthood. The stage was set after ten years of growth for a
rekindling of the fire of His first love and for a dedicated Christian

life style of servanthood that was called no more nor less than "normal Christian living." Challenges were set forth to enter new beginnings with an informed, seasoned love able to confront and exercise victory over cults, satanic forces as well as economic and cultural deprivations.

Along with these more mature and seasoned marks of Jesus' witness and love were the first gleanings that surround all conferences. Joyfully, there were people touched for the first time with Jesus' saving love. Father John Bertolucci once again was the Lord's powerful instrument in bringing first love to hearts melted away by the harrowing power of the Holy Spirit. Relationships were deeply healed and welded together, hearts tenderly lifted up a new song, broken bodies and bodies racked with pain were healed. The Lord blessed! Surely, He touched off brush fires that would burn and then kindle others for years to come. Alleluia!

He also spoke a prophetic word. He shared with His children on the first night of the conference that He "could not recognize His body." I'm not sure what this meant for others there but for me it signaled still another time when our Father expressed His mourning over our being separated in the body of Christ. The next day in a workshop led by Bob Mumford, Jake and myself, Jake reminded us all that, as a people, we had not been obedient to the prophetic words of Kansas City. When he asked the audience of some 5,000 people how many of their prayer groups at home had wept and mourned over the broken body of Christ, none raised their hands.

Our Father still calls us continually to try to "see" through His eyes and learn from His heart. He knows we live in very unusual times of challenge where the various calls He has issued may seem paradoxical and inconsistent to our minds. He is our one Father and Jesus is the Brother of us all. Without question and debate, we are one family, one body. Yet it appears that as we seek to be obedient to our particular denominational authority, we must somehow then compromise some other part of the body; as we lay down our lives for the noble, God-given call to love and submit to the brethren of our particular denominational leg of the body, we may lose track of our brethren outside of our denomination. There are subtle pressures: there are always those who become upset when we try to cross time-worn lines of division. Those who become upset are also the Father's children. We try to love them. But sometimes, in so doing, we back off from our deeper healing call to erase monumental division in order to preserve doctrinal purity.

David Wilkerson's vision points to a time when Catholic, Lutheran and other charismatic Christians will be faced with a decision. We will be called in our walk in the Spirit to bond together as the family of God, to exercise and nurture all the gifts of the Spirit, and to walk together as Christians baptized in the Spirit with pentecostal/charismatic understandings of what that means. Since some denominational leadership will turn against the use of gifts, the consequence may be a call out of denominational churches. The alternative choice is to remain obedient to church authority, give up the gifts and thus the movement and the fullness of the Holy Spirit today. This is a fearful prospect and, although I can imagine it happening, I surely don't want it to happen as I'm sure thousands of others don't. We need to share together the faith that we may still pray and beseech the Father in Jesus' name that this not come about. I believe if we do pray this, we must also then be willing to do two things. First, we must boldly pursue bridges of unity in the whole body for this indeed is our Father's plan. As we allow some of His heart to enter ours we will weep with Him that we are not one and, in this weeping, yearn for deeper unity and desire further that no harm will come to any brother or sister. Secondly, as we seek to do this in obedience and submission, I believe we all must more boldly challenge our leaders with the fullness of truth, for ultimately that's where the target of Wilkerson's vision lay. The Lord would only call His people out if His shepherds and leaders were unresponsive to the continued leadings of His Holy Spirit. It would be a sad day if we were all called to choose between the charismatic outpouring of the Holy Spirit today and our denominational authorities. In large part, this would only happen if we had some false concept of submission that became blind obedience rather than respectful and truthful disagreement if such were called upon.

It doesn't appear yet that Roman Catholics, in particular, are being called out of their churches or that such a choice is being presented them between their life in the Spirit and submission to their bishops if the New England Conference is to mean anything. As many as seventeen bishops attended, Cardinal Medeiros from Boston came, and as mentioned before, Pope John Paul II was present in spirit. Jesus was there. It was a glory-filled event!

Challenges came through the speakers who called for more servanthood in the church, more fire in the lives of her people, and more reaching out to the poor. A deeper challenge came prophetically, as mentioned before, from the Father who could not recognize His body. This prophetic challenge was emphasized through yet another occurrence. The Civic Center doors had been symbolically flung open to invite in the whole world and all men who would but give themselves to Jesus were invited to the Eucharistic table. Out into the streets of Providence did the warm hand of love extend to any and all in the name of Jesus to come to His banquet table. For a brief moment, I thought I was to go too, but then I remembered.

Something else must happen! The Lord is nurturing us to love one another. He has started something by His Spirit that no man can stop. He allows His children to make choices. I do not yet see the need for the drastic choice suggested in Wilkerson's vision. I do see, however, other choices of direction. One of these is to challenge and hold our leaders, shepherds and ourselves accountable to do all we can to bring together the body of Christ—today.